POEMS OF THE BRONTE SISTERS

BY CURRER, ELLIS, and ACTON BELL

(CHARLOTTE, EMILY and ANNE BRONTE)

A Digireads.com Book
Digireads.com Publishing

Poems of the Bronte Sisters
By Currer, Ellis, and Acton Bell (Charlotte, Emily, and Anne Bronte)
ISBN 10: 1-4209-4397-9
ISBN 13: 978-1-4209-4397-9

Please visit *www.digireads.com*

CONTENTS

POEMS BY CURRER BELL

POEMS BY ELLIS BELL

POEMS BY ACTON BELL

SELECTIONS FROM THE LITERARY REMAINS OF ELLIS AND ACTON BELL.

POEMS BY CURRER BELL

PILATE'S WIFE'S DREAM

I've quench'd my lamp, I struck it in that start
Which every limb convulsed, I heard it fall—
The crash blent with my sleep, I saw depart
Its light, even as I woke, on yonder wall;
Over against my bed, there shone a gleam
Strange, faint, and mingling also with my dream.

It sank, and I am wrapt in utter gloom;
How far is night advanced, and when will day
Retinge the dusk and livid air with bloom,
And fill this void with warm, creative ray?
Would I could sleep again till, clear and red,
Morning shall on the mountain-tops be spread!

I'd call my women, but to break their sleep,
Because my own is broken, were unjust;
They've wrought all day, and well-earn'd slumbers steep
Their labours in forgetfulness, I trust;
Let me my feverish watch with patience bear,
Thankful that none with me its sufferings share.

Yet, oh, for light! one ray would tranquillize
My nerves, my pulses, more than effort can;
I'll draw my curtain and consult the skies:
These trembling stars at dead of night look wan,
Wild, restless, strange, yet cannot be more drear
Than this my couch, shared by a nameless fear.

All black—one great cloud, drawn from east to west,
Conceals the heavens, but there are lights below;
Torches burn in Jerusalem, and cast
On yonder stony mount a lurid glow.
I see men station'd there, and gleaming spears;
A sound, too, from afar, invades my ears.

Dull, measured strokes of axe and hammer ring
From street to street, not loud, but through the night
Distinctly heard—and some strange spectral thing
Is now uprear'd—and, fix'd against the light
Of the pale lamps, defined upon that sky,
It stands up like a column, straight and high.

I see it all—I know the dusky sign—
A cross on Calvary, which Jews uprear
While Romans watch; and when the dawn shall shine
Pilate, to judge the victim, will appear—
Pass sentence-yield Him up to crucify;
And on that cross the spotless Christ must die.

Dreams, then, are true—for thus my vision ran;
Surely some oracle has been with me,
The gods have chosen me to reveal their plan,
To warn an unjust judge of destiny:
I, slumbering, heard and saw; awake I know,
Christ's coming death, and Pilate's life of woe.

I do not weep for Pilate—who could prove
Regret for him whose cold and crushing sway
No prayer can soften, no appeal can move:
Who tramples hearts as others trample clay,
Yet with a faltering, an uncertain tread,
That might stir up reprisal in the dead.

Forced to sit by his side and see his deeds;
Forced to behold that visage, hour by hour,
In whose gaunt lines the abhorrent gazer reads
A triple lust of gold, and blood, and power;
A soul whom motives fierce, yet abject, urge—
Rome's servile slave, and Judah's tyrant scourge.

How can I love, or mourn, or pity him?
I, who so long my fetter'd hands have wrung;
I, who for grief have wept my eyesight dim;
Because, while life for me was bright and young,
He robb'd my youth—he quench'd my life's fair ray—
He crush'd my mind, and did my freedom slay.

And at this hour-although I be his wife—
He has no more of tenderness from me
Than any other wretch of guilty life;
Less, for I know his household privacy—
I see him as he is—without a screen;
And, by the gods, my soul abhors his mien!

Has he not sought my presence, dyed in blood—
Innocent, righteous blood, shed shamelessly?
And have I not his red salute withstood?
Aye, when, as erst, he plunged all Galilee
In dark bereavement—in affliction sore,
Mingling their very offerings with their gore.

Then came he—in his eyes a serpent-smile,
Upon his lips some false, endearing word,
And through the streets of Salem clang'd the while
His slaughtering, hacking, sacrilegious sword—
And I, to see a man cause men such woe,
Trembled with ire—I did not fear to show.

And now, the envious Jewish priests have brought
Jesus—whom they in mock'ry call their king—
To have, by this grim power, their vengeance wrought;
By this mean reptile, innocence to sting.
Oh! could I but the purposed doom avert,
And shield the blameless head from cruel hurt!

Accessible is Pilate's heart to fear,
Omens will shake his soul, like autumn leaf;
Could he this night's appalling vision hear,
This just man's bonds were loosed, his life were safe,
Unless that bitter priesthood should prevail,
And make even terror to their malice quail.

Yet if I tell the dream—but let me pause.
What dream? Erewhile the characters were clear,
Graved on my brain—at once some unknown cause
Has dimm'd and razed the thoughts, which now appear,
Like a vague remnant of some by-past scene;—
Not what will be, but what, long since, has been.

I suffer'd many things—I heard foretold
A dreadful doom for Pilate,—lingering woes,
In far, barbarian climes, where mountains cold
Built up a solitude of trackless snows,
There he and grisly wolves prowl'd side by side,
There he lived famish'd—there, methought, he died;

But not of hunger, nor by malady;
I saw the snow around him, stain'd with gore;
I said I had no tears for such as he,
And, lo! my cheek is wet—mine eyes run o'er;
I weep for mortal suffering, mortal guilt,
I weep the impious deed, the blood self-spilt.

More I recall not, yet the vision spread
Into a world remote, an age to come—
And still the illumined name of Jesus shed
A light, a clearness, through the unfolding gloom—
And still I saw that sign, which now I see,
That cross on yonder brow of Calvary.

What is this Hebrew Christ?-to me unknown
His lineage—doctrine—mission; yet how clear
Is God-like goodness in his actions shown,
How straight and stainless is his life's career!
The ray of Deity that rests on him,
In my eyes makes Olympian glory dim.

The world advances; Greek or Roman rite
Suffices not the inquiring mind to stay;
The searching soul demands a purer light
To guide it on its upward, onward way;
Ashamed of sculptured gods, Religion turns
To where the unseen Jehovah's altar burns.

Our faith is rotten, all our rites defiled,
Our temples sullied, and, methinks, this man,
With his new ordinance, so wise and mild,
Is come, even as He says, the chaff to fan
And sever from the wheat; but will his faith
Survive the terrors of to-morrow's death?

* * * * * *

I feel a firmer trust—a higher hope
Rise in my soul—it dawns with dawning day;
Lo! on the Temple's roof—on Moriah's slope
Appears at length that clear and crimson ray
Which I so wished for when shut in by night;
Oh, opening skies, I hail, I bless pour light!

Part, clouds and shadows! Glorious Sun appear!
Part, mental gloom! Come insight from on high!
Dusk dawn in heaven still strives with daylight clear
The longing soul doth still uncertain sigh.
Oh! to behold the truth—that sun divine,
How doth my bosom pant, my spirit pine!

This day, Time travails with a mighty birth;
This day, Truth stoops from heaven and visits earth;
Ere night descends I shall more surely know
What guide to follow, in what path to go;
I wait in hope—I wait in solemn fear,
The oracle of God—the sole—true God—to hear.

MEMENTOS

Arranging long-locked drawers and shelves
Of cabinets, shut up for years,
What a strange task we've set ourselves!
How still the lonely room appears!
How strange this mass of ancient treasures,
Mementos of past pains and pleasures;
These volumes, clasped with costly stone,
With print all faded, gilding gone;

These fans of leaves from Indian trees—
These crimson shells, from Indian seas—
These tiny portraits, set in rings—
Once, doubtless, deemed such precious things;
Keepsakes bestowed by Love on Faith,
And worn till the receiver's death,
Now stored with cameos, china, shells,
In this old closet's dusty cells.

I scarcely think, for ten long years,
A hand has touched these relics old;
And, coating each, slow-formed, appears
The growth of green and antique mould.

All in this house is mossing over;
All is unused, and dim, and damp;
Nor light, nor warmth, the rooms discover—
Bereft for years of fire and lamp.

The sun, sometimes in summer, enters
The casements, with reviving ray;
But the long rains of many winters
Moulder the very walls away.

And outside all is ivy, clinging
To chimney, lattice, gable grey;
Scarcely one little red rose springing
Through the green moss can force its way.

Unscared, the daw and starling nestle,
Where the tall turret rises high,
And winds alone come near to rustle
The thick leaves where their cradles lie,

I sometimes think, when late at even
I climb the stair reluctantly,
Some shape that should be well in heaven,
Or ill elsewhere, will pass by me.

I fear to see the very faces,
Familiar thirty years ago,
Even in the old accustomed places
Which look so cold and gloomy now,

I've come, to close the window, hither,
At twilight, when the sun was down,
And Fear my very soul would wither,
Lest something should be dimly shown,

Too much the buried form resembling,
Of her who once was mistress here;
Lest doubtful shade, or moonbeam trembling,
Might take her aspect, once so dear.

Hers was this chamber; in her time
It seemed to me a pleasant room,
For then no cloud of grief or crime
Had cursed it with a settled gloom;

I had not seen death's image laid
In shroud and sheet, on yonder bed.
Before she married, she was blest—
Blest in her youth, blest in her worth;
Her mind was calm, its sunny rest
Shone in her eyes more clear than mirth.

And when attired in rich array,
Light, lustrous hair about her brow,
She yonder sat, a kind of day
Lit up what seems so gloomy now.
These grim oak walls even then were grim;
That old carved chair was then antique;
But what around looked dusk and dim
Served as a foil to her fresh cheek;
Her neck and arms, of hue so fair,
Eyes of unclouded, smiling light;
Her soft, and curled, and floating hair,
Gems and attire, as rainbow bright.

Reclined in yonder deep recess,
Ofttimes she would, at evening, lie
Watching the sun; she seemed to bless
With happy glance the glorious sky.
She loved such scenes, and as she gazed,
Her face evinced her spirit's mood;
Beauty or grandeur ever raised
In her, a deep-felt gratitude.
But of all lovely things, she loved
A cloudless moon, on summer night,
Full oft have I impatience proved
To see how long her still delight
Would find a theme in reverie,
Out on the lawn, or where the trees
Let in the lustre fitfully,
As their boughs parted momently,
To the soft, languid, summer breeze.
Alas! that she should e'er have flung
Those pure, though lonely joys away—
Deceived by false and guileful tongue,
She gave her hand, then suffered wrong;
Oppressed, ill-used, she faded young,
And died of grief by slow decay.

Open that casket-look how bright
Those jewels flash upon the sight;
The brilliants have not lost a ray
Of lustre, since her wedding day.
But see—upon that pearly chain—
How dim lies Time's discolouring stain!
I've seen that by her daughter worn:
For, ere she died, a child was born;—
A child that ne'er its mother knew,
That lone, and almost friendless grew;
For, ever, when its step drew nigh,

Averted was the father's eye;
And then, a life impure and wild
Made him a stranger to his child:
Absorbed in vice, he little cared
On what she did, or how she fared.
The love withheld she never sought,
She grew uncherished—learnt untaught;
To her the inward life of thought
Full soon was open laid.
I know not if her friendlessness
Did sometimes on her spirit press,
But plaint she never made.
The book-shelves were her darling treasure,
She rarely seemed the time to measure
    While she could read alone.
And she too loved the twilight wood
And often, in her mother's mood,
Away to yonder hill would hie,
Like her, to watch the setting sun,
Or see the stars born, one by one,
    Out of the darkening sky.
Nor would she leave that hill till night
Trembled from pole to pole with light;
Even then, upon her homeward way,
Long—long her wandering steps delayed
To quit the sombre forest shade,
Through which her eerie pathway lay.
You ask if she had beauty's grace?
I know not—but a nobler face
    My eyes have seldom seen;
A keen and fine intelligence,
And, better still, the truest sense
Were in her speaking mien.
But bloom or lustre was there none,
Only at moments, fitful shone
An ardour in her eye,
That kindled on her cheek a flush,
Warm as a red sky's passing blush
    And quick with energy.
Her speech, too, was not common speech,
No wish to shine, or aim to teach,
    Was in her words displayed:
She still began with quiet sense,
But oft the force of eloquence
    Came to her lips in aid;
Language and voice unconscious changed,
And thoughts, in other words arranged,
    Her fervid soul transfused

Into the hearts of those who heard,
And transient strength and ardour stirred,
   In minds to strength unused,
Yet in gay crowd or festal glare,
Grave and retiring was her air;
'Twas seldom, save with me alone,
That fire of feeling freely shone;
She loved not awe's nor wonder's gaze,
Nor even exaggerated praise,
Nor even notice, if too keen
The curious gazer searched her mien.
Nature's own green expanse revealed
The world, the pleasures, she could prize;
On free hill-side, in sunny field,
In quiet spots by woods concealed,
Grew wild and fresh her chosen joys,
Yet Nature's feelings deeply lay
In that endowed and youthful frame;
Shrined in her heart and hid from day,
They burned unseen with silent flame.
In youth's first search for mental light,
She lived but to reflect and learn,
But soon her mind's maturer might
For stronger task did pant and yearn;
And stronger task did fate assign,
Task that a giant's strength might strain;
To suffer long and ne'er repine,
Be calm in frenzy, smile at pain.

Pale with the secret war of feeling,
Sustained with courage, mute, yet high;
The wounds at which she bled, revealing
Only by altered cheek and eye;

She bore in silence—but when passion
Surged in her soul with ceaseless foam,
The storm at last brought desolation,
And drove her exiled from her home.

And silent still, she straight assembled
The wrecks of strength her soul retained;
For though the wasted body trembled,
The unconquered mind, to quail, disdained.

She crossed the sea—now lone she wanders
By Seine's, or Rhine's, or Arno's flow;
Fain would I know if distance renders
Relief or comfort to her woe.

Fain would I know if, henceforth, ever,
These eyes shall read in hers again,
That light of love which faded never,
Though dimmed so long with secret pain.

She will return, but cold and altered,
Like all whose hopes too soon depart;
Like all on whom have beat, unsheltered,
The bitter blasts that blight the heart.

No more shall I behold her lying
Calm on a pillow, smoothed by me;
No more that spirit, worn with sighing,
Will know the rest of infancy.

If still the paths of lore she follow,
'Twill be with tired and goaded will;
She'll only toil, the aching hollow,
The joyless blank of life to fill.

And oh! full oft, quite spent and weary,
Her hand will pause, her head decline;
That labor seems so hard and dreary,
On which no ray of hope may shine.

Thus the pale blight of time and sorrow
Will shade with grey her soft, dark hair;
Then comes the day that knows no morrow,
And death succeeds to long despair.

So speaks experience, sage and hoary;
I see it plainly, know it well,
Like one who, having read a story,
Each incident therein can tell.

Touch not that ring; 'twas his, the sire
    Of that forsaken child;
And nought his relics can inspire
    Save memories, sin-defiled.

I, who sat by his wife's death-bed,
    I, who his daughter loved,
Could almost curse the guilty dead,
    For woes the guiltless proved.

And heaven did curse—they found him laid,
   When crime for wrath was rife,
Cold—with the suicidal blade
Clutched in his desperate gripe.

'Twas near that long deserted hut,
Which in the wood decays,
Death's axe, self-wielded, struck his root,
And lopped his desperate days.

You know the spot, where three black trees,
Lift up their branches fell,
And moaning, ceaseless as the seas,
Still seem, in every passing breeze,
The deed of blood to tell.

They named him mad, and laid his bones
Where holier ashes lie;
Yet doubt not that his spirit groans
In hell's eternity.

But, lo! night, closing o'er the earth,
Infects our thoughts with gloom;
Come, let us strive to rally mirth
Where glows a clear and tranquil hearth
In some more cheerful room.

THE WIFE'S WILL

Sit still—a word—a breath may break
(As light airs stir a sleeping lake)
The glassy calm that soothes my woes—
The sweet, the deep, the full repose.
O leave me not! for ever be
Thus, more than life itself to me!

Yes, close beside thee let me kneel—
Give me thy hand, that I may feel
The friend so true—so tried—so dear,
My heart's own chosen—indeed is near;
And check me not—this hour divine
Belongs to me—is fully mine.

'Tis thy own hearth thou sitt'st beside,
After long absence—wandering wide;
'Tis thy own wife reads in thine eyes
A promise clear of stormless skies;
For faith and true love light the rays
Which shine responsive to her gaze.

Aye,—well that single tear may fall;
Ten thousand might mine eyes recall,
Which from their lids ran blinding fast,
In hours of grief, yet scarcely past;
Well mayst thou speak of love to me,
For, oh! most truly—I love thee!

Yet smile—for we are happy now.
Whence, then, that sadness on thy brow?
What sayst thou?" We muse once again,
Ere long, be severed by the main!"
I knew not this—I deemed no more
Thy step would err from Britain's shore.

"Duty commands!" 'Tis true—'tis just;
Thy slightest word I wholly trust,
Nor by request, nor faintest sigh,
Would I to turn thy purpose try;
But, William, hear my solemn vow—
Hear and confirm!—with thee I go.

"Distance and suffering," didst thou say?
"Danger by night, and toil by day?"
Oh, idle words and vain are these;
Hear me! I cross with thee the seas.
Such risk as thou must meet and dare,
I—thy true wife—will duly share.

Passive, at home, I will not pine;
Thy toils, thy perils shall be mine;
Grant this—and be hereafter paid
By a warm heart's devoted aid:
'Tis granted—with that yielding kiss,
Entered my soul unmingled bliss.

Thanks, William, thanks! thy love has joy,
Pure, undefiled with base alloy;
'Tis not a passion, false and blind,
Inspires, enchains, absorbs my mind;
Worthy, I feel, art thou to be
Loved with my perfect energy.

This evening now shall sweetly flow,
Lit by our clear fire's happy glow;
And parting's peace-embittering fear,
Is warned our hearts to come not near;
For fate admits my soul's decree,
In bliss or bale—to go with thee!

THE WOOD

But two miles more, and then we rest!
Well, there is still an hour of day,
And long the brightness of the West
Will light us on our devious way;
Sit then, awhile, here in this wood—
So total is the solitude,
   We safely may delay.

These massive roots afford a seat,
Which seems for weary travellers made.
There rest. The air is soft and sweet
In this sequestered forest glade,
And there are scents of flowers around,
The evening dew draws from the ground;
   How soothingly they spread!

Yes; I was tired, but not at heart;
No—that beats full of sweet content,
For now I have my natural part
Of action with adventure blent;
Cast forth on the wide world with thee,
And all my once waste energy
   To weighty purpose bent.

Yet—sayst thou, spies around us roam,
Our aims are termed conspiracy?
Haply, no more our English home
An anchorage for us may be?
That there is risk our mutual blood
May redden in some lonely wood
   The knife of treachery?

Sayst thou, that where we lodge each night,
In each lone farm, or lonelier hall
Of Norman Peer—ere morning light
Suspicion must as duly fall,
As day returns—such vigilance
Presides and watches over France,
 Such rigour governs all?

I fear not, William; dost thou fear?
So that the knife does not divide,
It may be ever hovering near:
I could not tremble at thy side,
And strenuous love—like mine for thee—
Is buckler strong 'gainst treachery,
 And turns its stab aside.

I am resolved that thou shalt learn
To trust my strength as I trust thine;
I am resolved our souls shall burn
With equal, steady, mingling shine;
Part of the field is conquered now,
Our lives in the same channel flow,
 Along the self-same line;

And while no groaning storm is heard,
Thou seem'st content it should be so,
But soon as comes a warning word
Of danger—straight thine anxious brow
Bends over me a mournful shade,
As doubting if my powers are made
 To ford the floods of woe.

Know, then it is my spirit swells,
And drinks, with eager joy, the air
Of freedom—where at last it dwells,
Chartered, a common task to share
With thee, and then it stirs alert,
And pants to learn what menaced hurt
 Demands for thee its care.

Remember, I have crossed the deep,
And stood with thee on deck, to gaze
On waves that rose in threatening heap,
While stagnant lay a heavy haze,
Dimly confusing sea with sky,
And baffling, even, the pilot's eye,
 Intent to thread the maze—

Of rocks, on Bretagne's dangerous coast,
And find a way to steer our band
To the one point obscure, which lost,
Flung us, as victims, on the strand;—
All, elsewhere, gleamed the Gallic sword,
And not a wherry could be moored
 Along the guarded land.

I feared not then—I fear not now;
The interest of each stirring scene
Wakes a new sense, a welcome glow,
In every nerve and bounding vein;
Alike on turbid Channel sea,
Or in still wood of Normandy,
 I feel as born again.

The rain descended that wild morn
When, anchoring in the cove at last,
Our band, all weary and forlorn
Ashore, like wave-worn sailors, cast—
Sought for a sheltering roof in vain,
And scarce could scanty food obtain
 To break their morning fast.

Thou didst thy crust with me divide,
Thou didst thy cloak around me fold;
And, sitting silent by thy side,
I ate the bread in peace untold:
Given kindly from thy hand, 'twas sweet
As costly fare or princely treat
 On royal plate of gold.

Sharp blew the sleet upon my face,
And, rising wild, the gusty wind
Drove on those thundering waves apace,
Our crew so late had left behind;
But, spite of frozen shower and storm,
So close to thee, my heart beat warm,
And tranquil slept my mind.

So now—nor foot-sore nor opprest
With walking all this August day,
I taste a heaven in this brief rest,
This gipsy-halt beside the way.
England's wild flowers are fair to view,
Like balm is England's summer dew
 Like gold her sunset ray.

But the white violets, growing here,
Are sweeter than I yet have seen,
And ne'er did dew so pure and clear
Distil on forest mosses green,
As now, called forth by summer heat,
Perfumes our cool and fresh retreat—
   These fragrant limes between.

That sunset! Look beneath the boughs,
Over the copse—beyond the hills;
How soft, yet deep and warm it glows,
And heaven with rich suffusion fills;
With hues where still the opal's tint,
Its gleam of prisoned fire is blent,
   Where flame through azure thrills!

Depart we now—for fast will fade
That solemn splendor of decline,
And deep must be the after-shade
As stars alone to-night will shine;
No moon is destined—pale—to gaze
On such a day's vast Phoenix blaze,
   A day in fires decayed!

There—hand-in-hand we tread again
The mazes of this varying wood,
And soon, amid a cultured plain,
Girt in with fertile solitude,
We shall our resting-place descry,
Marked by one roof-tree, towering high
   Above a farmstead rude.

Refreshed, erelong, with rustic fare,
We'll seek a couch of dreamless ease;
Courage will guard thy heart from fear,
And Love give mine divinest peace:
To-morrow brings more dangerous toil,
And through its conflict and turmoil
   We'll pass, as God shall please.

[*The preceding composition refers, doubtless, to the scenes acted in France during the last year of the Consulate.*]

FRANCES

She will not sleep, for fear of dreams,
But, rising, quits her restless bed,
And walks where some beclouded beams
Of moonlight through the hall are shed.

Obedient to the goad of grief,
Her steps, now fast, now lingering slow,
In varying motion seek relief
From the Eumenides of woe.

Wringing her hands, at intervals—
But long as mute as phantom dim—
She glides along the dusky walls,
Under the black oak rafters grim.

The close air of the grated tower
Stifles a heart that scarce can beat,
And, though so late and lone the hour,
Forth pass her wandering, faltering feet;

And on the pavement spread before
The long front of the mansion grey,
Her steps imprint the night-frost hoar,
Which pale on grass and granite lay.

Not long she stayed where misty moon
And shimmering stars could on her look,
But through the garden archway soon
Her strange and gloomy path she took.

Some firs, coeval with the tower,
Their straight black boughs stretched o'er her head;
Unseen, beneath this sable bower,
Rustled her dress and rapid tread.

There was an alcove in that shade,
Screening a rustic seat and stand;
Weary she sat her down, and laid
Her hot brow on her burning hand.

To solitude and to the night,
Some words she now, in murmurs, said;
And trickling through her fingers white,
Some tears of misery she shed.

"God help me in my grievous need,
God help me in my inward pain;
Which cannot ask for pity's meed,
Which has no licence to complain,

"Which must be borne; yet who can bear,
Hours long, days long, a constant weight—
The yoke of absolute despair,
A suffering wholly desolate?

"Who can for ever crush the heart,
Restrain its throbbing, curb its life?
Dissemble truth with ceaseless art,
With outward calm mask inward strife?"

She waited—as for some reply;
The still and cloudy night gave none;
Ere long, with deep-drawn, trembling sigh,
Her heavy plaint again begun.

"Unloved—I love; unwept—I weep;
Grief I restrain—hope I repress:
Vain is this anguish—fixed and deep;
Vainer, desires and dreams of bliss.

"My love awakes no love again,
My tears collect, and fall unfelt;
My sorrow touches none with pain,
My humble hopes to nothing melt.

"For me the universe is dumb,
Stone-deaf, and blank, and wholly blind;
Life I must bound, existence sum
In the strait limits of one mind;

"That mind my own. Oh! narrow cell;
Dark—imageless—a living tomb!
There must I sleep, there wake and dwell
Content, with palsy, pain, and gloom."

Again she paused; a moan of pain,
A stifled sob, alone was heard;
Long silence followed—then again
Her voice the stagnant midnight stirred.

"Must it be so? Is this my fate?
Can I nor struggle, nor contend?
And am I doomed for years to wait,
Watching death's lingering axe descend?

"And when it falls, and when I die,
What follows? Vacant nothingness?
The blank of lost identity?
Erasure both of pain and bliss?

"I've heard of heaven—I would believe;
For if this earth indeed be all,
Who longest lives may deepest grieve;
Most blest, whom sorrows soonest call.

"Oh! leaving disappointment here,
Will man find hope on yonder coast?
Hope, which, on earth, shines never clear,
And oft in clouds is wholly lost.

"Will he hope's source of light behold,
Fruition's spring, where doubts expire,
And drink, in waves of living gold,
Contentment, full, for long desire?

"Will he find bliss, which here he dreamed?
Rest, which was weariness on earth?
Knowledge, which, if o'er life it beamed,
Served but to prove it void of worth?

"Will he find love without lust's leaven,
Love fearless, tearless, perfect, pure,
To all with equal bounty given;
In all, unfeigned, unfailing, sure?

"Will he, from penal sufferings free,
Released from shroud and wormy clod,
All calm and glorious, rise and see
Creation's Sire—Existence' God?

"Then, glancing back on Time's brief woes,
Will he behold them, fading, fly;
Swept from Eternity's repose,
Like sullying cloud from pure blue sky?

"If so, endure, my weary frame;
And when thy anguish strikes too deep,
And when all troubled burns life's flame,
Think of the quiet, final sleep;

"Think of the glorious waking-hour,
Which will not dawn on grief and tears,
But on a ransomed spirit's power,
Certain, and free from mortal fears.

"Seek now thy couch, and lie till morn,
Then from thy chamber, calm, descend,
With mind nor tossed, nor anguish-torn,
But tranquil, fixed, to wait the end.

"And when thy opening eyes shall see
Mementos, on the chamber wall,
Of one who has forgotten thee,
Shed not the tear of acrid gall.

"The tear which, welling from the heart,
Burns where its drop corrosive falls,
And makes each nerve, in torture, start,
At feelings it too well recalls:

"When the sweet hope of being loved
Threw Eden sunshine on life's way:
When every sense and feeling proved
Expectancy of brightest day.

"When the hand trembled to receive
A thrilling clasp, which seemed so near,
And the heart ventured to believe
Another heart esteemed it dear.

"When words, half love, all tenderness,
Were hourly heard, as hourly spoken,
When the long, sunny days of bliss
Only by moonlight nights were broken.

"Till, drop by drop, the cup of joy
Filled full, with purple light was glowing,
And Faith, which watched it, sparkling high
Still never dreamt the overflowing.

"It fell not with a sudden crashing,
It poured not out like open sluice;
No, sparkling still, and redly flashing,
Drained, drop by drop, the generous juice.

"I saw it sink, and strove to taste it,
My eager lips approached the brim;
The movement only seemed to waste it;
It sank to dregs, all harsh and dim.

"These I have drunk, and they for ever
Have poisoned life and love for me;
A draught from Sodom's lake could never
More fiery, salt, and bitter, be.

"Oh! Love was all a thin illusion
Joy, but the desert's flying stream;
And glancing back on long delusion,
My memory grasps a hollow dream.

"Yet whence that wondrous change of feeling,
I never knew, and cannot learn;
Nor why my lover's eye, congealing,
Grew cold and clouded, proud and stern.

"Nor wherefore, friendship's forms forgetting,
He careless left, and cool withdrew;
Nor spoke of grief, nor fond regretting,
Nor ev'n one glance of comfort threw.

"And neither word nor token sending,
Of kindness, since the parting day,
His course, for distant regions bending,
Went, self-contained and calm, away.

"Oh, bitter, blighting, keen sensation,
Which will not weaken, cannot die,
Hasten thy work of desolation,
And let my tortured spirit fly!

"Vain as the passing gale, my crying;
Though lightning-struck, I must live on;
I know, at heart, there is no dying
Of love, and ruined hope, alone.

"Still strong and young, and warm with vigour,
Though scathed, I long shall greenly grow;
And many a storm of wildest rigour
Shall yet break o'er my shivered bough.

"Rebellious now to blank inertion,
My unused strength demands a task;
Travel, and toil, and full exertion,
Are the last, only boon I ask.

"Whence, then, this vain and barren dreaming
Of death, and dubious life to come?
I see a nearer beacon gleaming
Over dejection's sea of gloom.

"The very wildness of my sorrow
Tells me I yet have innate force;
My track of life has been too narrow,
Effort shall trace a broader course.

"The world is not in yonder tower,
Earth is not prisoned in that room,
'Mid whose dark panels, hour by hour,
I've sat, the slave and prey of gloom.

"One feeling—turned to utter anguish,
Is not my being's only aim;
When, lorn and loveless, life will languish,
But courage can revive the flame.

"He, when he left me, went a roving
To sunny climes, beyond the sea;
And I, the weight of woe removing,
Am free and fetterless as he.

"New scenes, new language, skies less clouded,
May once more wake the wish to live;
Strange, foreign towns, astir, and crowded,
New pictures to the mind may give.

"New forms and faces, passing ever,
May hide the one I still retain,
Defined, and fixed, and fading never,
Stamped deep on vision, heart, and brain.

"And we might meet—time may have changed him;
Chance may reveal the mystery,
The secret influence which estranged him;
Love may restore him yet to me.

"False thought—false hope—in scorn be banished!
I am not loved—nor loved have been;
Recall not, then, the dreams scarce vanished;
Traitors! mislead me not again!

"To words like yours I bid defiance,
'Tis such my mental wreck have made;
Of God alone, and self-reliance,
I ask for solace—hope for aid.

"Morn comes—and ere meridian glory
O'er these, my natal woods, shall smile,
Both lonely wood and mansion hoary
I'll leave behind, full many a mile."

GILBERT

I.—THE GARDEN

Above the city hung the moon,
    Right o'er a plot of ground
Where flowers and orchard-trees were fenced
    With lofty walls around:
'Twas Gilbert's garden—there to-night
    Awhile he walked alone;
And, tired with sedentary toil,
    Mused where the moonlight shone.

This garden, in a city-heart,
    Lay still as houseless wild,
Though many-windowed mansion fronts
    Were round it; closely piled;
But thick their walls, and those within
    Lived lives by noise unstirred;
Like wafting of an angel's wing,
    Time's flight by them was heard.

Some soft piano-notes alone
   Were sweet as faintly given,
Where ladies, doubtless, cheered the hearth
   With song that winter-even.
The city's many-mingled sounds
   Rose like the hum of ocean;
They rather lulled the heart than roused
   Its pulse to faster motion.

Gilbert has paced the single walk
   An hour, yet is not weary;
And, though it be a winter night
   He feels nor cold nor dreary.
The prime of life is in his veins,
   And sends his blood fast flowing,
And Fancy's fervour warms the thoughts
   Now in his bosom glowing.

Those thoughts recur to early love,
   Or what he love would name,
Though haply Gilbert's secret deeds
   Might other title claim.
Such theme not oft his mind absorbs,
   He to the world clings fast,
And too much for the present lives,
   To linger o'er the past.

But now the evening's deep repose
   Has glided to his soul;
That moonlight falls on Memory,
   And shows her fading scroll.
One name appears in every line
   The gentle rays shine o'er,
And still he smiles and still repeats
   That one name—Elinor.

There is no sorrow in his smile,
   No kindness in his tone;
The triumph of a selfish heart
   Speaks coldly there alone;
He says: "She loved me more than life;
   And truly it was sweet
To see so fair a woman kneel,
   In bondage, at my feet.

"There was a sort of quiet bliss
   To be so deeply loved,
To gaze on trembling eagerness
   And sit myself unmoved.
And when it pleased my pride to grant
   At last some rare caress,
To feel the fever of that hand
   My fingers deigned to press.

"'Twas sweet to see her strive to hide
   What every glance revealed;
Endowed, the while, with despot-might
   Her destiny to wield.
I knew myself no perfect man,
   Nor, as she deemed, divine;
I knew that I was glorious—but
   By her reflected shine;

"Her youth, her native energy,
   Her powers new-born and fresh,
'Twas these with Godhead sanctified
   My sensual frame of flesh.
Yet, like a god did I descend
   At last, to meet her love;
And, like a god, I then withdrew
   To my own heaven above.

"And never more could she invoke
   My presence to her sphere;
No prayer, no plaint, no cry of hers
   Could win my awful ear.
I knew her blinded constancy
   Would ne'er my deeds betray,
And, calm in conscience, whole in heart.
   I went my tranquil way.

"Yet, sometimes, I still feel a wish,
   The fond and flattering pain
Of passion's anguish to create
   In her young breast again.
Bright was the lustre of her eyes,
   When they caught fire from mine;
If I had power—this very hour,
   Again I'd light their shine.

"But where she is, or how she lives,
  I have no clue to know;
I've heard she long my absence pined,
  And left her home in woe.
But busied, then, in gathering gold,
  As I am busied now,
I could not turn from such pursuit,
  To weep a broken vow.

"Nor could I give to fatal risk
  The fame I ever prized;
Even now, I fear, that precious fame
  Is too much compromised."
An inward trouble dims his eye,
  Some riddle he would solve;
Some method to unloose a knot,
  His anxious thoughts revolve.

He, pensive, leans against a tree,
  A leafy evergreen,
The boughs, the moonlight, intercept,
  And hide him like a screen
He starts—the tree shakes with his tremor,
  Yet nothing near him pass'd;
He hurries up the garden alley,
  In strangely sudden haste.

With shaking hand, he lifts the latchet,
  Steps o'er the threshold stone;
The heavy door slips from his fingers—
  It shuts, and he is gone.
What touched, transfixed, appalled, his soul?—
  A nervous thought, no more;
'Twill sink like stone in placid pool,
  And calm close smoothly o'er.

II.—THE PARLOUR

Warm is the parlour atmosphere,
Serene the lamp's soft light;
The vivid embers, red and clear,
Proclaim a frosty night.
Books, varied, on the table lie,
Three children o'er them bend,
And all, with curious, eager eye,
The turning leaf attend.

Picture and tale alternately
Their simple hearts delight,
And interest deep, and tempered glee,
Illume their aspects bright.
The parents, from their fireside place,
Behold that pleasant scene,
And joy is on the mother's face,
Pride in the father's mien.

As Gilbert sees his blooming wife,
    Beholds his children fair,
No thought has he of transient strife,
    Or past, though piercing fear.
The voice of happy infancy
    Lisps sweetly in his ear,
His wife, with pleased and peaceful eye,
    Sits, kindly smiling, near.

The fire glows on her silken dress,
    And shows its ample grace,
And warmly tints each hazel tress,
    Curled soft around her face.
The beauty that in youth he wooed,
    Is beauty still, unfaded;
The brow of ever placid mood
    No churlish grief has shaded.

Prosperity, in Gilbert's home,
    Abides the guest of years;
There Want or Discord never come,
    And seldom Toil or Tears.
The carpets bear the peaceful print
    Of comfort's velvet tread,
And golden gleams, from plenty sent,
    In every nook are shed.

The very silken spaniel seems
    Of quiet ease to tell,
As near its mistress' feet it dreams,
    Sunk in a cushion's swell
And smiles seem native to the eyes
    Of those sweet children, three;
They have but looked on tranquil skies,
    And know not misery.

Alas! that Misery should come
    In such an hour as this;
Why could she not so calm a home
    A little longer miss?
But she is now within the door,
    Her steps advancing glide;
Her sullen shade has crossed the floor,
    She stands at Gilbert's side.

She lays her hand upon his heart,
    It bounds with agony;
His fireside chair shakes with the start
    That shook the garden tree.
His wife towards the children looks,
    She does not mark his mien;
The children, bending o'er their books,
    His terror have not seen.

In his own home, by his own hearth,
    He sits in solitude,
And circled round with light and mirth,
    Cold horror chills his blood.
His mind would hold with desperate clutch
    The scene that round him lies;
No—changed, as by some wizard's touch,
    The present prospect flies.

A tumult vague—a viewless strife
    His futile struggles crush;
'Twixt him and his an unknown life
    And unknown feelings rush.
He sees—but scarce can language paint
    The tissue fancy weaves;
For words oft give but echo faint
    Of thoughts the mind conceives.

Noise, tumult strange, and darkness dim,
    Efface both light and quiet;
No shape is in those shadows grim,
    No voice in that wild riot.
Sustain'd and strong, a wondrous blast
    Above and round him blows;
A greenish gloom, dense overcast,
    Each moment denser grows.

He nothing knows—nor clearly sees,
   Resistance checks his breath,
The high, impetuous, ceaseless breeze
   Blows on him cold as death.
And still the undulating gloom
   Mocks sight with formless motion:
Was such sensation Jonah's doom,
   Gulphed in the depths of ocean?

Streaking the air, the nameless vision,
   Fast-driven, deep-sounding, flows;
Oh! whence its source, and what its mission?
   How will its terrors close?
Long-sweeping, rushing, vast and void,
   The universe it swallows;
And still the dark, devouring tide
   A typhoon tempest follows.

More slow it rolls; its furious race
   Sinks to its solemn gliding;
The stunning roar, the wind's wild chase,
   To stillness are subsiding.
And, slowly borne along, a form
   The shapeless chaos varies;
Poised in the eddy to the storm,
   Before the eye it tarries.

A woman drowned—sunk in the deep,
   On a long wave reclining;
The circling waters' crystal sweep,
   Like glass, her shape enshrining.
Her pale dead face, to Gilbert turned,
   Seems as in sleep reposing;
A feeble light, now first discerned,
   The features well disclosing.

No effort from the haunted air
   The ghastly scene could banish,
That hovering wave, arrested there,
   Rolled—throbbed—but did not vanish.
If Gilbert upward turned his gaze,
   He saw the ocean-shadow;
If he looked down, the endless seas
   Lay green as summer meadow.

And straight before, the pale corpse lay,
   Upborne by air or billow,
So near, he could have touched the spray
   That churned around its pillow.
The hollow anguish of the face
   Had moved a fiend to sorrow;
Not death's fixed calm could rase the trace
   Of suffering's deep-worn furrow.

All moved; a strong returning blast,
   The mass of waters raising,
Bore wave and passive carcase past,
   While Gilbert yet was gazing.
Deep in her isle-conceiving womb,
   It seemed the ocean thundered,
And soon, by realms of rushing gloom,
   Were seer and phantom sundered.

Then swept some timbers from a wreck.
   On following surges riding;
Then sea-weed, in the turbid rack
   Uptorn, went slowly gliding.
The horrid shade, by slow degrees,
   A beam of light defeated,
And then the roar of raving seas,
   Fast, far, and faint, retreated.

And all was gone—gone like a mist,
   Corse, billows, tempest, wreck;
Three children close to Gilbert prest
   And clung around his neck.
Good night! good night! the prattlers said,
   And kissed their father's cheek;
'Twas now the hour their quiet bed
   And placid rest to seek.

The mother with her offspring goes
   To hear their evening prayer;
She nought of Gilbert's vision knows,
   And nought of his despair.
Yet, pitying God, abridge the time
   Of anguish, now his fate!
Though, haply, great has been his crime:
   Thy mercy, too, is great.

Gilbert, at length, uplifts his head,
  Bent for some moments low,
And there is neither grief nor dread
  Upon his subtle brow.
For well can he his feelings task,
  And well his looks command;
His features well his heart can mask,
  With smiles and smoothness bland.

Gilbert has reasoned with his mind—
  He says 'twas all a dream;
He strives his inward sight to blind
  Against truth's inward beam.
He pitied not that shadowy thing,
  When it was flesh and blood;
Nor now can pity's balmy spring
  Refresh his arid mood.

"And if that dream has spoken truth,"
  Thus musingly he says;
"If Elinor be dead, in sooth,
  Such chance the shock repays:
A net was woven round my feet,
  I scarce could further go;
Ere shame had forced a fast retreat,
  Dishonour brought me low.

"Conceal her, then, deep, silent sea,
  Give her a secret grave!
She sleeps in peace, and I am free,
  No longer terror's slave:
And homage still, from all the world,
  Shall greet my spotless name,
Since surges break and waves are curled
  Above its threatened shame."

III.—THE WELCOME HOME

Above the city hangs the moon,
  Some clouds are boding rain;
Gilbert, erewhile on journey gone,
  To-night comes home again.
Ten years have passed above his head,
  Each year has brought him gain;
His prosperous life has smoothly sped,
  Without or tear or stain.

'Tis somewhat late—the city clocks
   Twelve deep vibrations toll,
As Gilbert at the portal knocks,
   Which is his journey's goal.
The street is still and desolate,
   The moon hid by a cloud;
Gilbert, impatient, will not wait,—
   His second knock peals loud.

The clocks are hushed—there's not a light
   In any window nigh,
And not a single planet bright
   Looks from the clouded sky;
The air is raw, the rain descends,
   A bitter north-wind blows;
His cloak the traveller scarce defends—
   Will not the door unclose?

He knocks the third time, and the last
   His summons now they hear,
Within, a footstep, hurrying fast,
   Is heard approaching near.
The bolt is drawn, the clanking chain
   Falls to the floor of stone;
And Gilbert to his heart will strain
   His wife and children soon.

The hand that lifts the latchet, holds
   A candle to his sight,
And Gilbert, on the step, beholds
   A woman, clad in white.
Lo! water from her dripping dress
   Runs on the streaming floor;
From every dark and clinging tress
   The drops incessant pour.

There's none but her to welcome him;
   She holds the candle high,
And, motionless in form and limb,
   Stands cold and silent nigh;
There's sand and sea-weed on her robe,
   Her hollow eyes are blind;
No pulse in such a frame can throb,
   No life is there defined.

Gilbert turned ashy-white, but still
   His lips vouchsafed no cry;
He spurred his strength and master-will
   To pass the figure by,—
But, moving slow, it faced him straight,
   It would not flinch nor quail:
Then first did Gilbert's strength abate,
   His stony firmness quail.

He sank upon his knees and prayed
   The shape stood rigid there;
He called aloud for human aid,
   No human aid was near.
An accent strange did thus repeat
   Heaven's stern but just decree:
"The measure thou to her didst mete,
   To thee shall measured be!"

Gilbert sprang from his bended knees,
   By the pale spectre pushed,
And, wild as one whom demons seize,
   Up the hall-staircase rushed;
Entered his chamber—near the bed
   Sheathed steel and fire-arms hung—
Impelled by maniac purpose dread
   He chose those stores among.

Across his throat a keen-edged knife
   With vigorous hand he drew;
The wound was wide—his outraged life
   Rushed rash and redly through.
And thus died, by a shameful death,
   A wise and worldly man,
Who never drew but selfish breath
   Since first his life began.

LIFE

Life, believe, is not a dream
   So dark as sages say;
Oft a little morning rain
   Foretells a pleasant day.
Sometimes there are clouds of gloom,
   But these are transient all;
If the shower will make the roses bloom,
   O why lament its fall?
     Rapidly, merrily,

Life's sunny hours flit by,
　　Gratefully, cheerily
Enjoy them as they fly!
What though Death at times steps in,
　　And calls our Best away?
What though sorrow seems to win,
　　O'er hope, a heavy sway?
Yet Hope again elastic springs,
　　Unconquered, though she fell;
Still buoyant are her golden wings,
　　Still strong to bear us well.
　　　Manfully, fearlessly,
　　The day of trial bear,
　　　For gloriously, victoriously,
　　Can courage quell despair!

THE LETTER

What is she writing? Watch her now,
　　How fast her fingers move!
How eagerly her youthful brow
　　Is bent in thought above!
Her long curls, drooping, shade the light,
　　She puts them quick aside,
Nor knows that band of crystals bright,
　　Her hasty touch untied.
It slips adown her silken dress,
　　Falls glittering at her feet;
Unmarked it falls, for she no less
　　Pursues her labour sweet.

The very loveliest hour that shines,
　　Is in that deep blue sky;
The golden sun of June declines,
　　It has not caught her eye.
The cheerful lawn, and unclosed gate,
　　The white road, far away,
In vain for her light footsteps wait,
　　She comes not forth to-day.
There is an open door of glass
　　Close by that lady's chair,
From thence, to slopes of messy grass,
　　Descends a marble stair.

Tall plants of bright and spicy bloom
   Around the threshold grow;
Their leaves and blossoms shade the room
   From that sun's deepening glow.
Why does she not a moment glance
   Between the clustering flowers,
And mark in heaven the radiant dance
   Of evening's rosy hours?
O look again! Still fixed her eye,
   Unsmiling, earnest, still,
And fast her pen and fingers fly,
   Urged by her eager will.

Her soul is in th' absorbing task;
   To whom, then, doth she write?
Nay, watch her still more closely, ask
   Her own eyes' serious light;
Where do they turn, as now her pen
   Hangs o'er th' unfinished line?
Whence fell the tearful gleam that then
   Did in their dark spheres shine?
The summer-parlour looks so dark,
   When from that sky you turn,
And from th' expanse of that green park,
   You scarce may aught discern.

Yet, o'er the piles of porcelain rare,
   O'er flower-stand, couch, and vase,
Sloped, as if leaning on the air,
   One picture meets the gaze.
'Tis there she turns; you may not see
   Distinct, what form defines
The clouded mass of mystery
   Yon broad gold frame confines.
But look again; inured to shade
   Your eyes now faintly trace
A stalwart form, a massive head,
   A firm, determined face.

Black Spanish locks, a sunburnt cheek
   A brow high, broad, and white,
Where every furrow seems to speak
   Of mind and moral might.
Is that her god? I cannot tell;
   Her eye a moment met
Th' impending picture, then it fell
   Darkened and dimmed and wet.
A moment more, her task is done,
   And sealed the letter lies;
And now, towards the setting sun
   She turns her tearful eyes.

Those tears flow over, wonder not,
   For by the inscription see
In what a strange and distant spot
   Her heart of hearts must be!
Three seas and many a league of land
   That letter must pass o'er,
Ere read by him to whose loved hand
   'Tis sent from England's shore.
Remote colonial wilds detain
   Her husband, loved though stern;
She, 'mid that smiling English scene,
   Weeps for his wished return.

REGRET

Long ago I wished to leave
"The house where I was born;"
Long ago I used to grieve,
My home seemed so forlorn.
In other years, its silent rooms
Were filled with haunting fears;
Now, their very memory comes
O'ercharged with tender tears.

Life and marriage I have known.
Things once deemed so bright;
Now, how utterly is flown
Every ray of light!
'Mid the unknown sea, of life
I no blest isle have found;
At last, through all its wild wave's strife,
My bark is homeward bound.

Farewell, dark and rolling deep!
Farewell, foreign shore!
Open, in unclouded sweep,
Thou glorious realm before!
Yet, though I had safely pass'd
That weary, vexed main,
One loved voice, through surge and blast
Could call me back again.

Though the soul's bright morning rose
O'er Paradise for me,
William! even from Heaven's repose
I'd turn, invoked by thee!
Storm nor surge should e'er arrest
My soul, exalting then:
All my heaven was once thy breast,
Would it were mine again!

PRESENTIMENT

"Sister, you've sat there all the day,
    Come to the hearth awhile;
The wind so wildly sweeps away,
    The clouds so darkly pile.
That open book has lain, unread,
    For hours upon your knee;
You've never smiled nor turned your head;
    What can you, sister, see?"

"Come hither, Jane, look down the field;
    How dense a mist creeps on!
The path, the hedge, are both concealed,
    Ev'n the white gate is gone
No landscape through the fog I trace,
    No hill with pastures green;
All featureless is Nature's face.
    All masked in clouds her mien.

"Scarce is the rustle of a leaf
    Heard in our garden now;
The year grows old, its days wax brief,
    The tresses leave its brow.
The rain drives fast before the wind,
    The sky is blank and grey;
O Jane, what sadness fills the mind
    On such a dreary day!"

"You think too much, my sister dear;
  You sit too long alone;
What though November days be drear?
  Full soon will they be gone.
I've swept the hearth, and placed your chair.
  Come, Emma, sit by me;
Our own fireside is never drear,
Though late and wintry wane the year,
  Though rough the night may be."

"The peaceful glow of our fireside
  Imparts no peace to me:
My thoughts would rather wander wide
  Than rest, dear Jane, with thee.
I'm on a distant journey bound,
  And if, about my heart,
Too closely kindred ties were bound,
  'Twould break when forced to part.

"'Soon will November days be o'er:'
  Well have you spoken, Jane:
My own forebodings tell me more—
For me, I know by presage sure,
  They'll ne'er return again.
Ere long, nor sun nor storm to me
  Will bring or joy or gloom;
They reach not that Eternity
  Which soon will be my home."

Eight months are gone, the summer sun
  Sets in a glorious sky;
A quiet field, all green and lone,
  Receives its rosy dye.
Jane sits upon a shaded stile,
  Alone she sits there now;
Her head rests on her hand the while,
  And thought o'ercasts her brow.

She's thinking of one winter's day,
  A few short months ago,
Then Emma's bier was borne away
  O'er wastes of frozen snow.
She's thinking how that drifted snow
  Dissolved in spring's first gleam,
And how her sister's memory now
  Fades, even as fades a dream.

The snow will whiten earth again,
  But Emma comes no more;
She left, 'mid winter's sleet and rain,
  This world for Heaven's far shore.
On Beulah's hills she wanders now,
  On Eden's tranquil plain;
To her shall Jane hereafter go,
  She ne'er shall come to Jane!

THE TEACHER'S MONOLOGUE

The room is quiet, thoughts alone
People its mute tranquillity;
The yoke put off, the long task done,—
I am, as it is bliss to be,
Still and untroubled. Now, I see,
For the first time, how soft the day
O'er waveless water, stirless tree,
Silent and sunny, wings its way.
Now, as I watch that distant hill,
So faint, so blue, so far removed,
Sweet dreams of home my heart may fill,
That home where I am known and loved:
It lies beyond; yon azure brow
Parts me from all Earth holds for me;
And, morn and eve, my yearnings flow
Thitherward tending, changelessly.
My happiest hours, aye! all the time,
I love to keep in memory,
Lapsed among moors, ere life's first prime
Decayed to dark anxiety.

Sometimes, I think a narrow heart
Makes me thus mourn those far away,
And keeps my love so far apart
From friends and friendships of to-day;
Sometimes, I think 'tis but a dream
I treasure up so jealously,
All the sweet thoughts I live on seem
To vanish into vacancy:
And then, this strange, coarse world around
Seems all that's palpable and true;
And every sight, and every sound,
Combines my spirit to subdue
To aching grief, so void and lone
Is Life and Earth—so worse than vain,
The hopes that, in my own heart sown,

And cherished by such sun and rain
As Joy and transient Sorrow shed,
Have ripened to a harvest there:
Alas! methinks I hear it said,
"Thy golden sheaves are empty air."

All fades away; my very home
I think will soon be desolate;
I hear, at times, a warning come
Of bitter partings at its gate;
And, if I should return and see
The hearth-fire quenched, the vacant chair;
And hear it whispered mournfully,
That farewells have been spoken there,
What shall I do, and whither turn?
Where look for peace? When cease to mourn?

'Tis not the air I wished to play,
    The strain I wished to sing;
My wilful spirit slipped away
    And struck another string.
I neither wanted smile nor tear,
    Bright joy nor bitter woe,
But just a song that sweet and clear,
    Though haply sad, might flow.

A quiet song, to solace me
    When sleep refused to come;
A strain to chase despondency,
    When sorrowful for home.
In vain I try; I cannot sing;
    All feels so cold and dead;
No wild distress, no gushing spring
    Of tears in anguish shed;

But all the impatient gloom of one
    Who waits a distant day,
When, some great task of suffering done,
    Repose shall toil repay.
For youth departs, and pleasure flies,
    And life consumes away,
And youth's rejoicing ardour dies
    Beneath this drear delay;

And Patience, weary with her yoke,
   Is yielding to despair,
And Health's elastic spring is broke
   Beneath the strain of care.
Life will be gone ere I have lived;
   Where now is Life's first prime?
I've worked and studied, longed and grieved,
   Through all that rosy time.

To toil, to think, to long, to grieve,—
   Is such my future fate?
The morn was dreary, must the eve
   Be also desolate?
Well, such a life at least makes Death
   A welcome, wished-for friend;
Then, aid me, Reason, Patience, Faith,
   To suffer to the end!

PASSION

Some have won a wild delight,
   By daring wilder sorrow;
Could I gain thy love to-night,
   I'd hazard death to-morrow.

Could the battle-struggle earn
   One kind glance from thine eye,
How this withering heart would burn,
   The heady fight to try!

Welcome nights of broken sleep,
   And days of carnage cold,
Could I deem that thou wouldst weep
   To hear my perils told.

Tell me, if with wandering bands
   I roam full far away,
Wilt thou to those distant lands
   In spirit ever stray?

Wild, long, a trumpet sounds afar;
   Bid me—bid me go
Where Seik and Briton meet in war,
   On Indian Sutlej's flow.

Blood has dyed the Sutlej's waves
   With scarlet stain, I know;
Indus' borders yawn with graves,
   Yet, command me go!

Though rank and high the holocaust
   Of nations steams to heaven,
Glad I'd join the death-doomed host,
   Were but the mandate given.

Passion's strength should nerve my arm,
   Its ardour stir my life,
Till human force to that dread charm
Should yield and sink in wild alarm,
   Like trees to tempest-strife.

If, hot from war, I seek thy love,
   Darest thou turn aside?
Darest thou then my fire reprove,
   By scorn, and maddening pride?

No—my will shall yet control
   Thy will, so high and free,
And love shall tame that haughty soul—
   Yes—tenderest love for me.

I'll read my triumph in thine eyes,
   Behold, and prove the change;
Then leave, perchance, my noble prize,
   Once more in arms to range.

I'd die when all the foam is up,
   The bright wine sparkling high;
Nor wait till in the exhausted cup
   Life's dull dregs only lie.

Then Love thus crowned with sweet reward,
   Hope blest with fulness large,
I'd mount the saddle, draw the sword,
   And perish in the charge!

PREFERENCE

Not in scorn do I reprove thee,
Not in pride thy vows I waive,
But, believe, I could not love thee,
Wert thou prince, and I a slave.
These, then, are thine oaths of passion?
This, thy tenderness for me?
Judged, even, by thine own confession,
Thou art steeped in perfidy.
Having vanquished, thou wouldst leave me!
Thus I read thee long ago;
Therefore, dared I not deceive thee,
Even with friendship's gentle show.
Therefore, with impassive coldness
Have I ever met thy gaze;
Though, full oft, with daring boldness,
Thou thine eyes to mine didst raise.
Why that smile? Thou now art deeming
This my coldness all untrue,—
But a mask of frozen seeming,
Hiding secret fires from view.
Touch my hand, thou self-deceiver;
Nay-be calm, for I am so:
Does it burn? Does my lip quiver?
Has mine eye a troubled glow?
Canst thou call a moment's colour
To my forehead—to my cheek?
Canst thou tinge their tranquil pallor
With one flattering, feverish streak?
Am I marble? What! no woman
Could so calm before thee stand?
Nothing living, sentient, human,
Could so coldly take thy hand?
Yes—a sister might, a mother:
My good-will is sisterly:
Dream not, then, I strive to smother
Fires that inly burn for thee.
Rave not, rage not, wrath is fruitless,
Fury cannot change my mind;
I but deem the feeling rootless
Which so whirls in passion's wind.
Can I love? Oh, deeply—truly—
Warmly—fondly—but not thee;
And my love is answered duly,
With an equal energy.
Wouldst thou see thy rival? Hasten,

Draw that curtain soft aside,
Look where yon thick branches chasten
Noon, with shades of eventide.
In that glade, where foliage blending
Forms a green arch overhead,
Sits thy rival, thoughtful bending
O'er a stand with papers spread—
Motionless, his fingers plying
That untired, unresting pen;
Time and tide unnoticed flying,
There he sits—the first of men!
Man of conscience—man of reason;
Stern, perchance, but ever just;
Foe to falsehood, wrong, and treason,
Honour's shield, and virtue's trust!
Worker, thinker, firm defender
Of Heaven's truth—man's liberty;
Soul of iron—proof to slander,
Rock where founders tyranny.
Fame he seeks not—but full surely
She will seek him, in his home;
This I know, and wait securely
For the atoning hour to come.
To that man my faith is given,
Therefore, soldier, cease to sue;
While God reigns in earth and heaven,
I to him will still be true!

EVENING SOLACE

The human heart has hidden treasures,
In secret kept, in silence sealed;—
The thoughts, the hopes, the dreams, the pleasures,
Whose charms were broken if revealed.
And days may pass in gay confusion,
And nights in rosy riot fly,
While, lost in Fame's or Wealth's illusion,
The memory of the Past may die.

But there are hours of lonely musing,
Such as in evening silence come,
When, soft as birds their pinions closing,
The heart's best feelings gather home.
Then in our souls there seems to languish
A tender grief that is not woe;
And thoughts that once wrung groans of anguish
Now cause but some mild tears to flow.

And feelings, once as strong as passions,
Float softly back—a faded dream;
Our own sharp griefs and wild sensations,
The tale of others' sufferings seem.
Oh! when the heart is freshly bleeding,
How longs it for that time to be,
When, through the mist of years receding,
Its woes but live in reverie!

And it can dwell on moonlight glimmer,
On evening shade and loneliness;
And, while the sky grows dim and dimmer,
Feel no untold and strange distress—
Only a deeper impulse given
By lonely hour and darkened room,
To solemn thoughts that soar to heaven
Seeking a life and world to come.

STANZAS

If thou be in a lonely place,
    If one hour's calm be thine,
As Evening bends her placid face
    O'er this sweet day's decline;
If all the earth and all the heaven
    Now look serene to thee,
As o'er them shuts the summer even,
    One moment—think of me!

Pause, in the lane, returning home;
    'Tis dusk, it will be still:
Pause near the elm, a sacred gloom
    Its breezeless boughs will fill.
Look at that soft and golden light,
    High in the unclouded sky;
Watch the last bird's belated flight,
    As it flits silent by.

Hark! for a sound upon the wind,
    A step, a voice, a sigh;
If all be still, then yield thy mind,
    Unchecked, to memory.
If thy love were like mine, how blest
    That twilight hour would seem,
When, back from the regretted Past,
    Returned our early dream!

If thy love were like mine, how wild
   Thy longings, even to pain,
For sunset soft, and moonlight mild,
   To bring that hour again!
But oft, when in thine arms I lay,
   I've seen thy dark eyes shine,
And deeply felt their changeful ray
   Spoke other love than mine.

My love is almost anguish now,
   It beats so strong and true;
'Twere rapture, could I deem that thou
   Such anguish ever knew.
I have been but thy transient flower,
   Thou wert my god divine;
Till checked by death's congealing power,
   This heart must throb for thine.

And well my dying hour were blest,
   If life's expiring breath
Should pass, as thy lips gently prest
   My forehead cold in death;
And sound my sleep would be, and sweet,
   Beneath the churchyard tree,
If sometimes in thy heart should beat
   One pulse, still true to me.

PARTING

There's no use in weeping,
Though we are condemned to part:
There's such a thing as keeping
A remembrance in one's heart:

There's such a thing as dwelling
On the thought ourselves have nursed,
And with scorn and courage telling
The world to do its worst.

We'll not let its follies grieve us,
We'll just take them as they come;
And then every day will leave us
A merry laugh for home.

When we've left each friend and brother,
When we're parted wide and far,
We will think of one another,
As even better than we are.

Every glorious sight above us,
Every pleasant sight beneath,
We'll connect with those that love us,
Whom we truly love till death!

In the evening, when we're sitting
By the fire, perchance alone,
Then shall heart with warm heart meeting,
Give responsive tone for tone.

We can burst the bonds which chain us,
Which cold human hands have wrought,
And where none shall dare restrain us
We can meet again, in thought.

So there's no use in weeping,
Bear a cheerful spirit still;
Never doubt that Fate is keeping
Future good for present ill!

APOSTASY

This last denial of my faith,
   Thou, solemn Priest, hast heard;
And, though upon my bed of death,
   I call not back a word.
Point not to thy Madonna, Priest,—
   Thy sightless saint of stone;
She cannot, from this burning breast,
   Wring one repentant moan.

Thou say'st, that when a sinless child,
   I duly bent the knee,
And prayed to what in marble smiled
   Cold, lifeless, mute, on me.
I did. But listen! Children spring
   Full soon to riper youth;
And, for Love's vow and Wedlock's ring,
   I sold my early truth.

'Twas not a grey, bare head, like thine,
   Bent o'er me, when I said,
"That land and God and Faith are mine,
   For which thy fathers bled."
I see thee not, my eyes are dim;
   But well I hear thee say,
"O daughter cease to think of him
   Who led thy soul astray.

"Between you lies both space and time;
   Let leagues and years prevail
To turn thee from the path of crime,
   Back to the Church's pale."
And, did I need that, thou shouldst tell
   What mighty barriers rise
To part me from that dungeon-cell,
   Where my loved Walter lies?

And, did I need that thou shouldst taunt
   My dying hour at last,
By bidding this worn spirit pant
   No more for what is past?
Priest—*must* I cease to think of him?
   How hollow rings that word!
Can time, can tears, can distance dim
   The memory of my lord?

I said before, I saw not thee,
   Because, an hour agone,
Over my eyeballs, heavily,
   The lids fell down like stone.
But still my spirit's inward sight
   Beholds his image beam
As fixed, as clear, as burning bright,
   As some red planet's gleam.

Talk not of thy Last Sacrament,
   Tell not thy beads for me;
Both rite and prayer are vainly spent,
   As dews upon the sea.
Speak not one word of Heaven above,
   Rave not of Hell's alarms;
Give me but back my Walter's love,
   Restore me to his arms!

Then will the bliss of Heaven be won;
   Then will Hell shrink away,
As I have seen night's terrors shun
   The conquering steps of day.
'Tis my religion thus to love,
   My creed thus fixed to be;
Not Death shall shake, nor Priestcraft break
   My rock-like constancy!

Now go; for at the door there waits
   Another stranger guest;
He calls—I come—my pulse scarce beats,
   My heart fails in my breast.
Again that voice—how far away,
   How dreary sounds that tone!
And I, methinks, am gone astray
   In trackless wastes and lone.

I fain would rest a little while:
   Where can I find a stay,
Till dawn upon the hills shall smile,
   And show some trodden way?
"I come! I come!" in haste she said,
   "'Twas Walter's voice I heard!"
Then up she sprang—but fell back, dead,
   His name her latest word.

WINTER STORES

We take from life one little share,
   And say that this shall be
A space, redeemed from toil and care,
   From tears and sadness free.

And, haply, Death unstrings his bow,
   And Sorrow stands apart,
And, for a little while, we know
   The sunshine of the heart.

Existence seems a summer eve,
   Warm, soft, and full of peace,
Our free, unfettered feelings give
   The soul its full release.

A moment, then, it takes the power
   To call up thoughts that throw
Around that charmed and hallowed hour,
   This life's divinest glow.

But Time, though viewlessly it flies,
   And slowly, will not stay;
Alike, through clear and clouded skies,
   It cleaves its silent way.

Alike the bitter cup of grief,
   Alike the draught of bliss,
Its progress leaves but moment brief
   For baffled lips to kiss

The sparkling draught is dried away,
   The hour of rest is gone,
And urgent voices, round us, say,
   "Ho, lingerer, hasten on!"

And has the soul, then, only gained,
   From this brief time of ease,
A moment's rest, when overstrained,
   One hurried glimpse of peace?

No; while the sun shone kindly o'er us,
   And flowers bloomed round our feet,—
While many a bud of joy before us
   Unclosed its petals sweet,—

An unseen work within was plying;
   Like honey-seeking bee,
From flower to flower, unwearied, flying,
   Laboured one faculty,—

Thoughtful for Winter's future sorrow,
   Its gloom and scarcity;
Prescient to-day, of want to-morrow,
   Toiled quiet Memory.

'Tis she that from each transient pleasure
   Extracts a lasting good;
'Tis she that finds, in summer, treasure
   To serve for winter's food.

And when Youth's summer day is vanished,
   And Age brings Winter's stress,
Her stores, with hoarded sweets replenished,
   Life's evening hours will bless.

THE MISSIONARY

Plough, vessel, plough the British main,
Seek the free ocean's wider plain;
Leave English scenes and English skies,
Unbind, dissever English ties;
Bear me to climes remote and strange,
Where altered life, fast-following change,
Hot action, never-ceasing toil,
Shall stir, turn, dig, the spirit's soil;
Fresh roots shall plant, fresh seed shall sow,
Till a new garden there shall grow,
Cleared of the weeds that fill it now,—
Mere human love, mere selfish yearning,
Which, cherished, would arrest me yet.
I grasp the plough, there's no returning,
Let me, then, struggle to forget.

But England's shores are yet in view,
And England's skies of tender blue
Are arched above her guardian sea.
I cannot yet Remembrance flee;
I must again, then, firmly face
That task of anguish, to retrace.
Wedded to home—I home forsake;
Fearful of change—I changes make;
Too fond of ease—I plunge in toil;
Lover of calm—I seek turmoil:
Nature and hostile Destiny
Stir in my heart a conflict wild;
And long and fierce the war will be
Ere duty both has reconciled.

What other tie yet holds me fast
To the divorced, abandoned past?
Smouldering, on my heart's altar lies
The fire of some great sacrifice,
Not yet half quenched. The sacred steel
But lately struck my carnal will,
My life-long hope, first joy and last,
What I loved well, and clung to fast;
What I wished wildly to retain,

What I renounced with soul-felt pain;
What—when I saw it, axe-struck, perish—
Left me no joy on earth to cherish;
A man bereft—yet sternly now
I do confirm that Jephtha vow:
Shall I retract, or fear, or flee?
Did Christ, when rose the fatal tree
Before him, on Mount Calvary?
'Twas a long fight, hard fought, but won,
And what I did was justly done.

Yet, Helen! from thy love I turned,
When my heart most for thy heart burned;
I dared thy tears, I dared thy scorn—
Easier the death-pang had been borne.
Helen, thou mightst not go with me,
I could not—dared not stay for thee!
I heard, afar, in bonds complain
The savage from beyond the main;
And that wild sound rose o'er the cry
Wrung out by passion's agony;
And even when, with the bitterest tear
I ever shed, mine eyes were dim,
Still, with the spirit's vision clear,
I saw Hell's empire, vast and grim,
Spread on each Indian river's shore,
Each realm of Asia covering o'er.
There, the weak, trampled by the strong,
Live but to suffer—hopeless die;
There pagan-priests, whose creed is Wrong,
Extortion, Lust, and Cruelty,
Crush our lost race—and brimming fill
The bitter cup of human ill;
And I—who have the healing creed,
The faith benign of Mary's Son,
Shall I behold my brother's need,
And, selfishly, to aid him shun?
I—who upon my mother's knees,
In childhood, read Christ's written word,
Received his legacy of peace,
His holy rule of action heard;
I—in whose heart the sacred sense
Of Jesus' love was early felt;
Of his pure, full benevolence,
His pitying tenderness for guilt;
His shepherd-care for wandering sheep,
For all weak, sorrowing, trembling things,
His mercy vast, his passion deep

Of anguish for man's sufferings;
I—schooled from childhood in such lore—
Dared I draw back or hesitate,
When called to heal the sickness sore
Of those far off and desolate?
Dark, in the realm and shades of Death,
Nations, and tribes, and empires lie,
But even to them the light of Faith
Is breaking on their sombre sky:
And be it mine to bid them raise
Their drooped heads to the kindling scene,
And know and hail the sunrise blaze
Which heralds Christ the Nazarene.
I know how Hell the veil will spread
Over their brows and filmy eyes,
And earthward crush the lifted head
That would look up and seek the skies;
I know what war the fiend will wage
Against that soldier of the Cross,
Who comes to dare his demon rage,
And work his kingdom shame and loss.
Yes, hard and terrible the toil
Of him who steps on foreign soil,
Resolved to plant the gospel vine,
Where tyrants rule and slaves repine;
Eager to lift Religion's light
Where thickest shades of mental night
Screen the false god and fiendish rite;
Reckless that missionary blood,
Shed in wild wilderness and wood,
Has left, upon the unblest air,
The man's deep moan—the martyr's prayer.
I know my lot—I only ask
Power to fulfil the glorious task;
Willing the spirit, may the flesh
Strength for the day receive afresh.
May burning sun or deadly wind
Prevail not o'er an earnest mind;
May torments strange or direst death
Nor trample truth, nor baffle faith.
Though such blood-drops should fall from me
As fell in old Gethsemane,
Welcome the anguish, so it gave
More strength to work—more skill to save.
And, oh! if brief must be my time,
If hostile hand or fatal clime
Cut short my course—still o'er my grave,
Lord, may thy harvest whitening wave.

So I the culture may begin,
Let others thrust the sickle in;
If but the seed will faster grow,
May my blood water what I sow!

What! have I ever trembling stood,
And feared to give to God that blood?
What! has the coward love of life
Made me shrink from the righteous strife?
Have human passions, human fears
Severed me from those Pioneers
Whose task is to march first, and trace
Paths for the progress of our race?
It has been so; but grant me, Lord,
Now to stand steadfast by Thy word!
Protected by salvation's helm,
Shielded by faith, with truth begirt,
To smile when trials seek to whelm
And stand mid testing fires unhurt!
Hurling hell's strongest bulwarks down,
Even when the last pang thrills my breast,
When death bestows the martyr's crown,
And calls me into Jesus' rest.
Then for my ultimate reward—
Then for the world-rejoicing word—
The voice from Father—Spirit—Son:
"Servant of God, well hast thou done!"

POEMS BY ELLIS BELL

FAITH AND DESPONDENCY

"The winter wind is loud and wild,
Come close to me, my darling child;
Forsake thy books, and mateless play;
And, while the night is gathering gray,
We'll talk its pensive hours away;—

   "Iernë, round our sheltered hall
November's gusts unheeded call;
Not one faint breath can enter here
Enough to wave my daughter's hair,
And I am glad to watch the blaze
Glance from her eyes, with mimic rays;
To feel her cheek, so softly pressed,
In happy quiet on my breast,

"But, yet, even this tranquillity
Brings bitter, restless thoughts to me;
And, in the red fire's cheerful glow,
I think of deep glens, blocked with snow;
I dream of moor, and misty hill,
Where evening closes dark and chill;
For, lone, among the mountains cold,
Lie those that I have loved of old.
And my heart aches, in hopeless pain,
Exhausted with repinings vain,
That I shall greet them ne'er again!"

"Father, in early infancy,
When you were far beyond the sea,
Such thoughts were tyrants over me!
I often sat, for hours together,
Through the long nights of angry weather,
Raised on my pillow, to descry
The dim moon struggling in the sky;
Or, with strained ear, to catch the shock,
Of rock with wave, and wave with rock;
So would I fearful vigil keep,
And, all for listening, never sleep.
But this world's life has much to dread,
Not so, my Father, with the dead.

"Oh! not for them, should we despair,
The grave is drear, but they are not there;
Their dust is mingled with the sod,
Their happy souls are gone to God!
You told me this, and yet you sigh,
And murmur that your friends must die.
Ah! my dear father, tell me why?
For, if your former words were true,
How useless would such sorrow be;
As wise, to mourn the seed which grew
Unnoticed on its parent tree,
Because it fell in fertile earth,
And sprang up to a glorious birth—
Struck deep its root, and lifted high
Its green boughs in the breezy sky.

"But, I'll not fear, I will not weep
For those whose bodies rest in sleep,—
I know there is a blessed shore,
   Opening its ports for me and mine;
And, gazing Time's wide waters o'er,
   I weary for that land divine,
Where we were born, where you and I
Shall meet our dearest, when we die;
From suffering and corruption free,
Restored into the Deity."

"Well hast thou spoken, sweet, trustful child!
   And wiser than thy sire;
And worldly tempests, raging wild,
   Shall strengthen thy desire—
Thy fervent hope, through storm and foam,
   Through wind and ocean's roar,
To reach, at last, the eternal home,
   The steadfast, changeless shore!"

STARS

Ah! why, because the dazzling sun
   Restored our Earth to joy,
Have you departed, every one,
   And left a desert sky?

All through the night, your glorious eyes
   Were gazing down in mine,
And, with a full heart's thankful sighs,
   I blessed that watch divine.

I was at peace, and drank your beams
   As they were life to me;
And revelled in my changeful dreams,
   Like petrel on the sea.

Thought followed thought, star followed star,
   Through boundless regions, on;
While one sweet influence, near and far,
   Thrilled through, and proved us one!

Why did the morning dawn to break
   So great, so pure, a spell;
And scorch with fire the tranquil cheek,
   Where your cool radiance fell?

Blood-red, he rose, and, arrow-straight,
   His fierce beams struck my brow;
The soul of nature sprang, elate,
   But *mine* sank sad and low!

My lids closed down, yet through their veil
   I saw him, blazing, still,
And steep in gold the misty dale,
   And flash upon the hill.

I turned me to the pillow, then,
   To call back night, and see
Your worlds of solemn light, again,
   Throb with my heart, and me!

It would not do—the pillow glowed,
   And glowed both roof and floor;
And birds sang loudly in the wood,
   And fresh winds shook the door;

The curtains waved, the wakened flies
   Were murmuring round my room,
Imprisoned there, till I should rise,
   And give them leave to roam.

Oh, stars, and dreams, and gentle night;
   Oh, night and stars, return!
And hide me from the hostile light
   That does not warm, but burn;

That drains the blood of suffering men;
   Drinks tears, instead of dew;
Let me sleep through his blinding reign,
   And only wake with you!

THE PHILOSOPHER

Enough of thought, philosopher!
   Too long hast thou been dreaming
Unlightened, in this chamber drear,
   While summer's sun is beaming!
Space-sweeping soul, what sad refrain
Concludes thy musings once again?

"Oh, for the time when I shall sleep
Without identity.
And never care how rain may steep,
Or snow may cover me!
No promised heaven, these wild desires
Could all, or half fulfil;
No threatened hell, with quenchless fires,
Subdue this quenchless will!"

"So said I, and still say the same;
    Still, to my death, will say—
Three gods, within this little frame,
    Are warring night; and day;
Heaven could not hold them all, and yet
    They all are held in me;
And must be mine till I forget
    My present entity!
Oh, for the time, when in my breast
    Their struggles will be o'er!
Oh, for the day, when I shall rest,
    And never suffer more!"

"I saw a spirit, standing, man,
    Where thou dost stand—an hour ago,
And round his feet three rivers ran,
    Of equal depth, and equal flow—
A golden stream—and one like blood;
    And one like sapphire seemed to be;
But, where they joined their triple flood
    It tumbled in an inky sea
The spirit sent his dazzling gaze
    Down through that ocean's gloomy night;
Then, kindling all, with sudden blaze,
    The glad deep sparkled wide and bright—
White as the sun, far, far more fair
    Than its divided sources were!"

"And even for that spirit, seer,
    I've watched and sought my life-time long;
Sought him in heaven, hell, earth, and air,
    An endless search, and always wrong.
Had I but seen his glorious eye
    Once light the clouds that wilder me;
I ne'er had raised this coward cry
    To cease to think, and cease to be;

I ne'er had called oblivion blest,
   Nor stretching eager hands to death,
Implored to change for senseless rest
   This sentient soul, this living breath—
Oh, let me die—that power and will
   Their cruel strife may close;
And conquered good, and conquering ill
   Be lost in one repose!"

REMEMBRANCE

Cold in the earth—and the deep snow piled above thee,
Far, far, removed, cold in the dreary grave!
Have I forgot, my only Love, to love thee,
Severed at last by Time's all-severing wave?

Now, when alone, do my thoughts no longer hover
Over the mountains, on that northern shore,
Resting their wings where heath and fern-leaves cover
Thy noble heart for ever, ever more?

Cold in the earth—and fifteen wild Decembers,
From those brown hills, have melted into spring:
Faithful, indeed, is the spirit that remembers
After such years of change and suffering!

Sweet Love of youth, forgive, if I forget thee,
While the world's tide is bearing me along;
Other desires and other hopes beset me,
Hopes which obscure, but cannot do thee wrong!

No later light has lightened up my heaven,
No second morn has ever shone for me;
All my life's bliss from thy dear life was given,
All my life's bliss is in the grave with thee.

But, when the days of golden dreams had perished,
And even Despair was powerless to destroy;
Then did I learn how existence could be cherished,
Strengthened, and fed without the aid of joy.

Then did I check the tears of useless passion—
Weaned my young soul from yearning after thine;
Sternly denied its burning wish to hasten
Down to that tomb already more than mine.

And, even yet, I dare not let it languish,
Dare not indulge in memory's rapturous pain;
Once drinking deep of that divinest anguish,
How could I seek the empty world again?

A DEATH-SCENE

"O day! he cannot die
When thou so fair art shining!
O Sun, in such a glorious sky,
So tranquilly declining;

He cannot leave thee now,
While fresh west winds are blowing,
And all around his youthful brow
Thy cheerful light is glowing!

Edward, awake, awake—
The golden evening gleams
Warm and bright on Arden's lake—
Arouse thee from thy dreams!

Beside thee, on my knee,
My dearest friend, I pray
That thou, to cross the eternal sea,
Wouldst yet one hour delay:

I hear its billows roar—
I see them foaming high;
But no glimpse of a further shore
Has blest my straining eye.

Believe not what they urge
Of Eden isles beyond;
Turn back, from that tempestuous surge,
To thy own native land.

It is not death, but pain
That struggles in thy breast—
Nay, rally, Edward, rouse again;
I cannot let thee rest!"

One long look, that sore reproved me
For the woe I could not bear—
One mute look of suffering moved me
To repent my useless prayer:

And, with sudden check, the heaving
Of distraction passed away;
Not a sign of further grieving
Stirred my soul that awful day.

Paled, at length, the sweet sun setting;
Sunk to peace the twilight breeze:
Summer dews fell softly, wetting
Glen, and glade, and silent trees.

Then his eyes began to weary,
Weighed beneath a mortal sleep;
And their orbs grew strangely dreary,
Clouded, even as they would weep.

But they wept not, but they changed not,
Never moved, and never closed;
Troubled still, and still they ranged not—
Wandered not, nor yet reposed!

So I knew that he was dying—
Stooped, and raised his languid head;
Felt no breath, and heard no sighing,
So I knew that he was dead.

SONG

The linnet in the rocky dells,
    The moor-lark in the air,
The bee among the heather bells
    That hide my lady fair:

The wild deer browse above her breast;
    The wild birds raise their brood;
And they, her smiles of love caressed,
    Have left her solitude!

I ween, that when the grave's dark wall
    Did first her form retain,
They thought their hearts could ne'er recall
    The light of joy again.

They thought the tide of grief would flow
    Unchecked through future years;
But where is all their anguish now,
    And where are all their tears?

Well, let them fight for honour's breath,
   Or pleasure's shade pursue—
The dweller in the land of death
   Is changed and careless too.

And, if their eyes should watch and weep
   Till sorrow's source were dry,
She would not, in her tranquil sleep,
   Return a single sigh!

Blow, west-wind, by the lonely mound,
   And murmur, summer-streams—
There is no need of other sound
   To soothe my lady's dreams.

ANTICIPATION

How beautiful the earth is still,
To thee—how full of happiness?
How little fraught with real ill,
Or unreal phantoms of distress!
How spring can bring thee glory, yet,
And summer win thee to forget
   December's sullen time!
Why dost thou hold the treasure fast,
Of youth's delight, when youth is past,
   And thou art near thy prime?

When those who were thy own compeers,
Equals in fortune and in years,
Have seen their morning melt in tears,
   To clouded, smileless day;
Blest, had they died untried and young,
Before their hearts went wandering wrong,—
Poor slaves, subdued by passions strong,
   A weak and helpless prey!

'Because, I hoped while they enjoyed,
And by fulfilment, hope destroyed;
As children hope, with trustful breast,
I waited bliss—and cherished rest.
A thoughtful spirit taught me soon,
That we must long till life be done;
That every phase of earthly joy
Must always fade, and always cloy:

'This I foresaw—and would not chase
The fleeting treacheries;
But, with firm foot and tranquil face,
Held backward from that tempting race,
Gazed o'er the sands the waves efface,
   To the enduring seas—
There cast my anchor of desire
Deep in unknown eternity;
Nor ever let my spirit tire,
With looking for *what is to be!*

"It is hope's spell that glorifies,
Like youth, to my maturer eyes,
All Nature's million mysteries,
   The fearful and the fair—
Hope soothes me in the griefs I know;
She lulls my pain for others' woe,
And makes me strong to undergo
   What I am born to bear.

Glad comforter! will I not brave,
Unawed, the darkness of the grave?
Nay, smile to hear Death's billows rave—
   Sustained, my guide, by thee?
The more unjust seems present fate,
The more my spirit swells elate,
Strong, in thy strength, to anticipate
   Rewarding destiny!

THE PRISONER

A FRAGMENT

In the dungeon-crypts idly did I stray,
Reckless of the lives wasting there away;
"Draw the ponderous bars! open, Warder stern!"
He dared not say me nay—the hinges harshly turn.

"Our guests are darkly lodged," I whisper'd, gazing through
The vault, whose grated eye showed heaven more gray than blue;
(This was when glad Spring laughed in awaking pride;)
"Aye, darkly lodged enough!" returned my sullen guide.

Then, God forgive my youth; forgive my careless tongue;
I scoffed, as the chill chains on the damp flagstones rung:
"Confined in triple walls, art thou so much to fear,
That we must bind thee down and clench thy fetters here?"

The captive raised her face; it was as soft and mild
As sculptured marble saint, or slumbering unwean'd child;
It was so soft and mild, it was so sweet and fair,
Pain could not trace a line, nor grief a shadow there!

The captive raised her hand and pressed it to her brow;
"I have been struck," she said, "and I am suffering now;
Yet these are little worth, your bolts and irons strong;
And, were they forged in steel, they could not hold me long."

Hoarse laughed the jailor grim: "Shall I be won to hear;
Dost think, fond, dreaming wretch, that *I* shall grant thy prayer?
Or, better still, wilt melt my master's heart with groans?
Ah! sooner might the sun thaw down these granite stones.

"My master's voice is low, his aspect bland and kind,
But hard as hardest flint the soul that lurks behind;
And I am rough and rude, yet not more rough to see
Than is the hidden ghost that has its home in me."

About her lips there played a smile of almost scorn,
"My friend," she gently said, "you have not heard me mourn;
When you my kindred's lives, *my* lost life, can restore,
Then may I weep and sue,—but never, friend, before!

"Still, let my tyrants know, I am not doomed to wear
Year after year in gloom, and desolate despair;
A messenger of Hope comes every night to me,
And offers for short life, eternal liberty.

"He comes with western winds, with evening's wandering airs,
With that clear dusk of heaven that brings the thickest stars.
Winds take a pensive tone, and stars a tender fire,
And visions rise, and change, that kill me with desire.

"Desire for nothing known in my maturer years,
When Joy grew mad with awe, at counting future tears.
When, if my spirit's sky was full of flashes warm,
I knew not whence they came, from sun or thunder-storm.

"But, first, a hush of peace—a soundless calm descends;
The struggle of distress, and fierce impatience ends;
Mute music soothes my breast—unuttered harmony,
That I could never dream, till Earth was lost to me.

"Then dawns the Invisible; the Unseen its truth reveals;
My outward sense is gone, my inward essence feels:
Its wings are almost free—its home, its harbour found,
Measuring the gulph, it stoops and dares the final bound,

"Oh I dreadful is the check—intense the agony—
When the ear begins to hear, and the eye begins to see;
When the pulse begins to throb, the brain to think again;
The soul to feel the flesh, and the flesh to feel the chain.

"Yet I would lose no sting, would wish no torture less;
The more that anguish racks, the earlier it will bless;
And robed in fires of hell, or bright with heavenly shine,
If it but herald death, the vision is divine!"

She ceased to speak, and we, unanswering, turned to go—
We had no further power to work the captive woe:
Her cheek, her gleaming eye, declared that man had given
A sentence, unapproved, and overruled by Heaven.

HOPE

Hope was but a timid friend;
   She sat without the grated den,
Watching how my fate would tend,
   Even as selfish-hearted men.

She was cruel in her fear;
   Through the bars one dreary day,
I looked out to see her there,
   And she turned her face away!

Like a false guard, false watch keeping,
   Still, in strife, she whispered peace;
She would sing while I was weeping;
   If I listened, she would cease.

False she was, and unrelenting;
   When my last joys strewed the ground,
Even Sorrow saw, repenting,
   Those sad relics scattered round;

Hope, whose whisper would have given
   Balm to all my frenzied pain,
Stretched her wings, and soared to heaven,
   Went, and ne'er returned again!

A DAY DREAM

On a sunny brae alone I lay
   One summer afternoon;
It was the marriage-time of May,
   With her young lover, June.

From her mother's heart seemed loath to part
   That queen of bridal charms,
But her father smiled on the fairest child
   He ever held in his arms.

The trees did wave their plumy crests,
   The glad birds carolled clear;
And I, of all the wedding guests,
   Was only sullen there!

There was not one, but wished to shun
   My aspect void of cheer;
The very gray rocks, looking on,
   Asked, "What do you here?"

And I could utter no reply;
   In sooth, I did not know
Why I had brought a clouded eye
   To greet the general glow.

So, resting on a heathy bank,
   I took my heart to me;
And we together sadly sank
   Into a reverie.

We thought, "When winter comes again,
   Where will these bright things be?
All vanished, like a vision vain,
   An unreal mockery!

"The birds that now so blithely sing,
   Through deserts, frozen dry,
Poor spectres of the perished spring,
   In famished troops will fly.

"And why should we be glad at all?
   The leaf is hardly green,
Before a token of its fall
   Is on the surface seen!"

Now, whether it were really so,
   I never could be sure;
But as in fit of peevish woe,
   I stretched me on the moor,

A thousand thousand gleaming fires
   Seemed kindling in the air;
A thousand thousand silvery lyres
   Resounded far and near:

Methought, the very breath I breathed
   Was full of sparks divine,
And all my heather-couch was wreathed
   By that celestial shine!

And, while the wide earth echoing rung
   To that strange minstrelsy
The little glittering spirits sung,
   Or seemed to sing, to me:

"O mortal! mortal! let them die;
   Let time and tears destroy,
That we may overflow the sky
   With universal joy!

"Let grief distract the sufferer's breast,
   And night obscure his way;
They hasten him to endless rest,
   And everlasting day.

"To thee the world is like a tomb,
   A desert's naked shore;
To us, in unimagined bloom,
   It brightens more and more!

"And, could we lift the veil, and give
   One brief glimpse to thine eye,
Thou wouldst rejoice for those that live,
   Because they live to die."

The music ceased; the noonday dream,
   Like dream of night, withdrew;
But Fancy, still, will sometimes deem
   Her fond creation true.

TO IMAGINATION

When weary with the long day's care,
   And earthly change from pain to pain,
And lost, and ready to despair,
   Thy kind voice calls me back again:
Oh, my true friend! I am not lone,
While thou canst speak with such a tone!

So hopeless is the world without;
   The world within I doubly prize;
Thy world, where guile, and hate, and doubt,
   And cold suspicion never rise;
Where thou, and I, and Liberty,
Have undisputed sovereignty.

What matters it, that all around
   Danger, and guilt, and darkness lie,
If but within our bosom's bound
   We hold a bright, untroubled sky,
Warm with ten thousand mingled rays
Of suns that know no winter days?

Reason, indeed, may oft complain
   For Nature's sad reality,
And tell the suffering heart how vain
   Its cherished dreams must always be;
And Truth may rudely trample down
The flowers of Fancy, newly-blown:

But thou art ever there, to bring
   The hovering vision back, and breathe
New glories o'er the blighted spring,
   And call a lovelier Life from Death.
And whisper, with a voice divine,
Of real worlds, as bright as thine.

I trust not to thy phantom bliss,
   Yet, still, in evening's quiet hour,
With never-failing thankfulness,
   I welcome thee, Benignant Power;
Sure solacer of human cares,
And sweeter hope, when hope despairs!

HOW CLEAR SHE SHINES

How clear she shines! How quietly
   I lie beneath her guardian light;
While heaven and earth are whispering me,
   "To morrow, wake, but dream to-night."
Yes, Fancy, come, my Fairy love!
   These throbbing temples softly kiss;
And bend my lonely couch above,
   And bring me rest, and bring me bliss.

The world is going; dark world, adieu!
   Grim world, conceal thee till the day;
The heart thou canst not all subdue
Must still resist, if thou delay!

Thy love I will not, will not share;
   Thy hatred only wakes a smile;
Thy griefs may wound—thy wrongs may tear,
   But, oh, thy lies shall ne'er beguile!
While gazing on the stars that glow
   Above me, in that stormless sea,
I long to hope that all the woe
   Creation knows, is held in thee!

And this shall be my dream to-night;
   I'll think the heaven of glorious spheres
Is rolling on its course of light
   In endless bliss, through endless years;
I'll think, there's not one world above,
   Far as these straining eyes can see,
Where Wisdom ever laughed at Love,
   Or Virtue crouched to Infamy;

Where, writing 'neath the strokes of Fate,
   The mangled wretch was forced to smile;
To match his patience 'gainst her hate,
   His heart rebellious all the while.
Where Pleasure still will lead to wrong,
   And helpless Reason warn in vain;
And Truth is weak, and Treachery strong;
   And Joy the surest path to Pain;
And Peace, the lethargy of Grief;
   And Hope, a phantom of the soul;
And life, a labour, void and brief;
   And Death, the despot of the whole!

SYMPATHY

There should be no despair for you
   While nightly stars are burning;
While evening pours its silent dew,
   And sunshine gilds the morning.
There should be no despair—though tears
   May flow down like a river:
Are not the best beloved of years
   Around your heart for ever?

They weep, you weep, it must be so;
   Winds sigh as you are sighing,
And winter sheds its grief in snow
   Where Autumn's leaves are lying:
Yet, these revive, and from their fate
   Your fate cannot be parted:
Then, journey on, if not elate,
   Still, *never* broken-hearted!

PLEAD FOR ME

Oh, thy bright eyes must answer now,
When Reason, with a scornful brow,
Is mocking at my overthrow!
Oh, thy sweet tongue must plead for me
And tell why I have chosen thee!

Stern Reason is to judgment come,
Arrayed in all her forms of gloom:
Wilt thou, my advocate, be dumb?
No, radiant angel, speak and say,
Why I did cast the world away.

Why I have persevered to shun
The common paths that others run;
And on a strange road journeyed on,
Heedless, alike of wealth and power—
Of glory's wreath and pleasure's flower.

These, once, indeed, seemed Beings Divine;
And they, perchance, heard vows of mine,
And saw my offerings on their shrine;
But careless gifts are seldom prized,
And *mine* were worthily despised.

So, with a ready heart, I swore
To seek their altar-stone no more;
And gave my spirit to adore
Thee, ever-present, phantom thing—
My slave, my comrade, and my king.

A slave, because I rule thee still;
Incline thee to my changeful will,
And make thy influence good or ill:
A comrade, for by day and night
Thou art my intimate delight,—

My darling pain that wounds and sears,
And wrings a blessing out from tears
By deadening me to earthly cares;
And yet, a king, though Prudence well
Have taught thy subject to rebel

And am I wrong to worship where
Faith cannot doubt, nor hope despair,
Since my own soul can grant my prayer?
Speak, God of visions, plead for me,
And tell why I have chosen thee!

SELF-INTEROGATION

"The evening passes fast away.
    'Tis almost time to rest;
What thoughts has left the vanished day,
    What feelings in thy breast?

"The vanished day? It leaves a sense
    Of labour hardly done;
Of little gained with vast expense—
    A sense of grief alone?

"Time stands before the door of Death,
   Upbraiding bitterly
And Conscience, with exhaustless breath,
   Pours black reproach on me:

"And though I've said that Conscience lies
   And Time should Fate condemn;
Still, sad Repentance clouds my eyes,
   And makes me yield to them!

"Then art thou glad to seek repose?
   Art glad to leave the sea,
And anchor all thy weary woes
   In calm Eternity?

"Nothing regrets to see thee go—
   Not one voice sobs' farewell;'
And where thy heart has suffered so,
   Canst thou desire to dwell?"

"Alas! the countless links are strong
   That bind us to our clay;
The loving spirit lingers long,
   And would not pass away!

"And rest is sweet, when laurelled fame
   Will crown the soldier's crest;
But a brave heart, with a tarnished name,
   Would rather fight than rest.

"Well, thou hast fought for many a year,
   Hast fought thy whole life through,
Hast humbled Falsehood, trampled Fear;
   What is there left to do?

"'Tis true, this arm has hotly striven,
   Has dared what few would dare;
Much have I done, and freely given,
   But little learnt to bear!

"Look on the grave where thou must sleep
   Thy last, and strongest foe;
It is endurance not to weep,
   If that repose seem woe.

"The long war closing in defeat—
   Defeat serenely borne,—
Thy midnight rest may still be sweet,
   And break in glorious morn!"

DEATH

Death! that struck when I was most confiding.
   In my certain faith of joy to be—
Strike again, Time's withered branch dividing
   From the fresh root of Eternity!

Leaves, upon Time's branch, were growing brightly,
   Full of sap, and full of silver dew;
Birds beneath its shelter gathered nightly;
   Daily round its flowers the wild bees flew.

Sorrow passed, and plucked the golden blossom;
   Guilt stripped off the foliage in its pride
But, within its parent's kindly bosom,
   Flowed for ever Life's restoring tide.

Little mourned I for the parted gladness,
   For the vacant nest and silent song—
Hope was there, and laughed me out of sadness;
   Whispering, "Winter will not linger long!"

And, behold! with tenfold increase blessing,
   Spring adorned the beauty-burdened spray;
Wind and rain and fervent heat, caressing,
   Lavished glory on that second May!

High it rose—no winged grief could sweep it;
   Sin was scared to distance with its shine;
Love, and its own life, had power to keep it
   From all wrong—from every blight but thine!

Cruel Death! The young leaves droop and languish;
   Evening's gentle air may still restore—
No! the morning sunshine mocks my anguish-
   Time, for me, must never blossom more!

Strike it down, that other boughs may flourish
   Where that perished sapling used to be;
Thus, at least, its mouldering corpse will nourish
   That from which it sprung—Eternity.

STANZAS TO ——

Well, some may hate, and some may scorn,
And some may quite forget thy name;
But my sad heart must ever mourn
Thy ruined hopes, thy blighted fame!
'Twas thus I thought, an hour ago,
Even weeping o'er that wretch's woe;
One word turned back my gushing tears,
And lit my altered eye with sneers.
Then "Bless the friendly dust," I said,
"That hides thy unlamented head!
Vain as thou wert, and weak as vain,
The slave of Falsehood, Pride, and Pain—
My heart has nought akin to thine;
Thy soul is powerless over mine."
But these were thoughts that vanished too;
Unwise, unholy, and untrue:
Do I despise the timid deer,
Because his limbs are fleet with fear?
Or, would I mock the wolf's death-howl,
Because his form is gaunt and foul?
Or, hear with joy the leveret's cry,
Because it cannot bravely die?
No! Then above his memory
Let Pity's heart as tender be;
Say, "Earth, lie lightly on that breast,
And, kind Heaven, grant that spirit rest!"

HONOUR'S MARTYR

The moon is full this winter night;
    The stars are clear, though few;
And every window glistens bright
    With leaves of frozen dew.

The sweet moon through your lattice gleams,
    And lights your room like day;
And there you pass, in happy dreams,
    The peaceful hours away!

While I, with effort hardly quelling
    The anguish in my breast,
Wander about the silent dwelling,
    And cannot think of rest.

The old clock in the gloomy hall
   Ticks on, from hour to hour;
And every time its measured call
   Seems lingering slow and slower:

And, oh, how slow that keen-eyed star
   Has tracked the chilly gray!
What, watching yet! how very far
   The morning lies away!

Without your chamber door I stand;
   Love, are you slumbering still?
My cold heart, underneath my hand,
   Has almost ceased to thrill.

Bleak, bleak the east wind sobs and sighs,
   And drowns the turret bell,
Whose sad note, undistinguished, dies
   Unheard, like my farewell!

To-morrow, Scorn will blight my name,
   And Hate will trample me,
Will load me with a coward's shame—
   A traitor's perjury.

False friends will launch their covert sneers;
   True friends will wish me dead;
And I shall cause the bitterest tears
   That you have ever shed.

The dark deeds of my outlawed race
   Will then like virtues shine;
And men will pardon their disgrace,
   Beside the guilt of mine.

For, who forgives the accursed crime
   Of dastard treachery?
Rebellion, in its chosen time,
   May Freedom's champion be;

Revenge may stain a righteous sword,
   It may be just to slay;
But, traitor, traitor,—from *that* word
   All true breasts shrink away!

Oh, I would give my heart to death,
  To keep my honour fair;
Yet, I'll not give my inward faith
  My honour's *name* to spare!

Not even to keep your priceless love,
  Dare I, Beloved, deceive;
This treason should the future prove,
  Then, only then, believe!

I know the path I ought to go
  I follow fearlessly,
Inquiring not what deeper woe
  Stern duty stores for me.

So foes pursue, and cold allies
  Mistrust me, every one:
Let me be false in others' eyes,
  If faithful in my own.

STANZAS

I'll not weep that thou art going to leave me,
There's nothing lovely here;
And doubly will the dark world grieve me,
While thy heart suffers there.

I'll not weep, because the summer's glory
Must always end in gloom;
And, follow out the happiest story—
It closes with a tomb!

And I am weary of the anguish
Increasing winters bear;
Weary to watch the spirit languish
Through years of dead despair.

So, if a tear, when thou art dying,
Should haply fall from me,
It is but that my soul is sighing,
To go and rest with thee.

MY COMFORTER

Well hast thou spoken, and yet not taught
   A feeling strange or new;
Thou hast but roused a latent thought,
A cloud-closed beam of sunshine brought
   To gleam in open view.

Deep down, concealed within my soul,
   That light lies hid from men;
Yet glows unquenched—though shadows roll,
Its gentle ray cannot control—
   About the sullen den.

Was I not vexed, in these gloomy ways
   To walk alone so long?
Around me, wretches uttering praise,
Or howling o'er their hopeless days,
   And each with Frenzy's tongue;—

A brotherhood of misery,
   Their smiles as sad as sighs;
Whose madness daily maddened me,
Distorting into agony
   The bliss before my eyes!

So stood I, in Heaven's glorious sun,
   And in the glare of Hell;
My spirit drank a mingled tone,
Of seraph's song, and demon's moan;
What my soul bore, my soul alone
   Within itself may tell!

Like a soft, air above a sea,
   Tossed by the tempest's stir;
A thaw-wind, melting quietly
The snow-drift on some wintry lea;
No: what sweet thing resembles thee,
   My thoughtful Comforter?

And yet a little longer speak,
   Calm this resentful mood;
And while the savage heart grows meek,
For other token do not seek,
But let the tear upon my cheek
   Evince my gratitude!

THE OLD STOIC

Riches I hold in light esteem,
    And Love I laugh to scorn;
And lust of fame was but a dream,
    That vanished with the morn:

And if I pray, the only prayer
    That moves my lips for me
Is, "Leave the heart that now I bear,
    And give me liberty!"

Yes, as my swift days near their goal:
    'Tis all that I implore;
In life and death a chainless soul,
    With courage to endure.

POEMS BY ACTON BELL

A REMINISCENCE

Yes, thou art gone! and never more
Thy sunny smile shall gladden me;
But I may pass the old church door,
And pace the floor that covers thee,

May stand upon the cold, damp stone,
And think that, frozen, lies below
The lightest heart that I have known,
The kindest I shall ever know.

Yet, though I cannot see thee more,
'Tis still a comfort to have seen;
And though thy transient life is o'er,
'Tis sweet to think that thou hast been;

To think a soul so near divine,
Within a form so angel fair,
United to a heart like thine,
Has gladdened once our humble sphere.

THE ARBOUR

I'll rest me in this sheltered bower,
And look upon the clear blue sky
That smiles upon me through the trees,
Which stand so thick clustering by;

And view their green and glossy leaves,
All glistening in the sunshine fair;
And list the rustling of their boughs,
So softly whispering through the air.

And while my ear drinks in the sound,
My winged soul shall fly away;
Reviewing lone departed years
As one mild, beaming, autumn day;

And soaring on to future scenes,
Like hills and woods, and valleys green,
All basking in the summer's sun,
But distant still, and dimly seen.

Oh, list! 'tis summer's very breath
That gently shakes the rustling trees—
But look! the snow is on the ground—
How can I think of scenes like these?

'Tis but the *frost* that clears the air,
And gives the sky that lovely blue;
They're smiling in a *winter's* sun,
Those evergreens of sombre hue.

And winter's chill is on my heart—
How can I dream of future bliss?
How can my spirit soar away,
Confined by such a chain as this?

HOME

How brightly glistening in the sun
   The woodland ivy plays!
While yonder beeches from their barks
   Reflect his silver rays.

That sun surveys a lovely scene
   From softly smiling skies;
And wildly through unnumbered trees
   The wind of winter sighs:

Now loud, it thunders o'er my head,
   And now in distance dies.
But give me back my barren hills
   Where colder breezes rise;

Where scarce the scattered, stunted trees
   Can yield an answering swell,
But where a wilderness of heath
   Returns the sound as well.

For yonder garden, fair and wide,
   With groves of evergreen,
Long winding walks, and borders trim,
   And velvet lawns between;

Restore to me that little spot,
   With gray walls compassed round,
Where knotted grass neglected lies,
   And weeds usurp the ground.

Though all around this mansion high
   Invites the foot to roam,
And though its halls are fair within—
   Oh, give me back my *home*!

VANITAS VANITATUM, OMNIA VANITAS

In all we do, and hear, and see,
Is restless Toil and Vanity.
While yet the rolling earth abides,
Men come and go like ocean tides;

And ere one generation dies,
Another in its place shall rise;
That, sinking soon into the grave,
Others succeed, like wave on wave;

And as they rise, they pass away.
The sun arises every day,
And hastening onward to the West,
He nightly sinks, but not to rest:

Returning to the eastern skies,
Again to light us, he must rise.
And still the restless wind comes forth,
Now blowing keenly from the North;

Now from the South, the East, the West,
For ever changing, ne'er at rest.
The fountains, gushing from the hills,
Supply the ever-running rills;

The thirsty rivers drink their store,
And bear it rolling to the shore,
But still the ocean craves for more.
'Tis endless labour everywhere!
Sound cannot satisfy the ear,

Light cannot fill the craving eye,
Nor riches half our wants supply,
Pleasure but doubles future pain,
And joy brings sorrow in her train;

Laughter is mad, and reckless mirth—
What does she in this weary earth?
Should Wealth, or Fame, our Life employ,
Death comes, our labour to destroy;

To snatch the untasted cup away,
For which we toiled so many a day.
What, then, remains for wretched man?
To use life's comforts while he can,

Enjoy the blessings Heaven bestows,
Assist his friends, forgive his foes;
Trust God, and keep His statutes still,
Upright and firm, through good and ill;

Thankful for all that God has given,
Fixing his firmest hopes on Heaven;
Knowing that earthly joys decay,
But hoping through the darkest day.

THE PENITENT

I mourn with thee, and yet rejoice
   That thou shouldst sorrow so;
With angel choirs I join my voice
   To bless the sinner's woe.

Though friends and kindred turn away,
   And laugh thy grief to scorn;
I hear the great Redeemer say,
   "Blessed are ye that mourn."

Hold on thy course, nor deem it strange
   That earthly cords are riven:
Man may lament the wondrous change,
   But "there is joy in heaven!"

MUSIC ON CHRISTMAS MORNING

Music I love—but never strain
Could kindle raptures so divine,
So grief assuage, so conquer pain,
And rouse this pensive heart of mine—
As that we hear on Christmas morn,
Upon the wintry breezes borne.

Though Darkness still her empire keep,
And hours must pass, ere morning break;
From troubled dreams, or slumbers deep,
That music *kindly* bids us wake:
It calls us, with an angel's voice,
To wake, and worship, and rejoice;

To greet with joy the glorious morn,
Which angels welcomed long ago,
When our redeeming Lord was born,
To bring the light of Heaven below;
The Powers of Darkness to dispel,
And rescue Earth from Death and Hell.

While listening to that sacred strain,
My raptured spirit soars on high;
I seem to hear those songs again
Resounding through the open sky,
That kindled such divine delight,
In those who watched their flocks by night.

With them I celebrate His birth—
Glory to God, in highest Heaven,
Good-will to men, and peace on earth,
To us a Saviour-king is given;
Our God is come to claim His own,
And Satan's power is overthrown!

A sinless God, for sinful men,
Descends to suffer and to bleed;
Hell *must* renounce its empire then;
The price is paid, the world is freed,
And Satan's self must now confess
That Christ has earned a *right* to bless:

Now holy Peace may smile from heaven,
And heavenly Truth from earth shall spring:
The captive's galling bonds are riven,
For our Redeemer is our king;
And He that gave his blood for men
Will lead us home to God again.

STANZAS

Oh, weep not, love! each tear that springs
    In those dear eyes of thine,
To me a keener suffering brings
    Than if they flowed from mine.

And do not droop! however drear
    The fate awaiting thee;
For *my* sake combat pain and care,
    And cherish life for me!

I do not fear thy love will fail;
    Thy faith is true, I know;
But, oh, my love! thy strength is frail
    For such a life of woe.

Were 't not for this, I well could trace
    (Though banished long from thee)
Life's rugged path, and boldly face
    The storms that threaten me.

Fear not for me—I've steeled my mind
    Sorrow and strife to greet;
Joy with my love I leave behind,
    Care with my friends I meet.

A mother's sad reproachful eye,
   A father's scowling brow—
But he may frown and she may sigh:
   I will not break my vow!

I love my mother, I revere
   My sire, but fear not me—
Believe that Death alone can tear
   This faithful heart from thee.

IF THIS BE ALL

O God! if this indeed be all
   That Life can show to me;
If on my aching brow may fall
   No freshening dew from Thee;

If with no brighter light than this
   The lamp of hope may glow,
And I may only *dream* of bliss,
   And wake to weary woe;

If friendship's solace must decay,
   When other joys are gone,
And love must keep so far away,
   While I go wandering on,—

Wandering and toiling without gain,
   The slave of others' will,
With constant care, and frequent pain,
   Despised, forgotten still;

Grieving to look on vice and sin,
   Yet powerless to quell
The silent current from within,
   The outward torrent's swell

While all the good I would impart,
   The feelings I would share,
Are driven backward to my heart,
   And turned to wormwood there;

If clouds must *ever* keep from sight
   The glories of the Sun,
And I must suffer Winter's blight,
   Ere Summer is begun;

If Life must be so full of care,
   Then call me soon to thee;
Or give me strength enough to bear
   My load of misery.

MEMORY

Brightly the sun of summer shone
Green fields and waving woods upon,
   And soft winds wandered by;
Above, a sky of purest blue,
Around, bright flowers of loveliest hue,
   Allured the gazer's eye.

But what were all these charms to me,
When one sweet breath of memory
   Came gently wafting by?
I closed my eyes against the day,
And called my willing soul away,
   From earth, and air, and sky;

That I might simply fancy there
One little flower—a primrose fair,
   Just opening into sight;
As in the days of infancy,
An opening primrose seemed to me
   A source of strange delight.

Sweet Memory! ever smile on me;
Nature's chief beauties spring from thee;
   Oh, still thy tribute bring
Still make the golden crocus shine
Among the flowers the most divine,
   The glory of the spring.

Still in the wallflower's fragrance dwell;
And hover round the slight bluebell,
   My childhood's darling flower.
Smile on the little daisy still,
The buttercup's bright goblet fill
   With all thy former power.

For ever hang thy dreamy spell
Round mountain star and heather bell,
   And do not pass away
From sparkling frost, or wreathed snow,
And whisper when the wild winds blow,
   Or rippling waters play.

Is childhood, then, so all divine?
Or Memory, is the glory thine,
   That haloes thus the past?
Not *all* divine; its pangs of grief
(Although, perchance, their stay be brief)
   Are bitter while they last.

Nor is the glory all thine own,
For on our earliest joys alone
   That holy light is cast.
With such a ray, no spell of thine
Can make our later pleasures shine,
   Though long ago they passed.

TO COWPER

Sweet are thy strains, celestial Bard;
   And oft, in childhood's years,
I've read them o'er and o'er again,
   With floods of silent tears.

The language of my inmost heart
   I traced in every line;
My sins, *my* sorrows, hopes, and fears,
   Were there-and only mine.

All for myself the sigh would swell,
   The tear of anguish start;
I little knew what wilder woe
   Had filled the Poet's heart.

I did not know the nights of gloom,
   The days of misery;
The long, long years of dark despair,
   That crushed and tortured thee.

But they are gone; from earth at length
   Thy gentle soul is pass'd,
And in the bosom of its God
   Has found its home at last.

It must be so, if God is love,
　And answers fervent prayer;
Then surely thou shalt dwell on high,
　And I may meet thee there.

Is He the source of every good,
　The spring of purity?
Then in thine hours of deepest woe,
　Thy God was still with thee.

How else, when every hope was fled,
　Couldst thou so fondly cling
To holy things and help men?
　And how so sweetly sing,

Of things that God alone could teach?
　And whence that purity,
That hatred of all sinful ways—
　That gentle charity?

Are *these* the symptoms of a heart
　Of heavenly grace bereft—
For ever banished from its God,
　To Satan's fury left?

Yet, should thy darkest fears be true,
　If Heaven be so severe,
That such a soul as thine is lost,—
　Oh! how shall *I* appear?

THE DOUBTER'S PRAYER

Eternal Power, of earth and air!
Unseen, yet seen in all around,
Remote, but dwelling everywhere,
Though silent, heard in every sound;

If e'er thine ear in mercy bent,
When wretched mortals cried to Thee,
And if, indeed, Thy Son was sent,
To save lost sinners such as me:

Then hear me now, while kneeling here,
I lift to thee my heart and eye,
And all my soul ascends in prayer,
Oh, give me—give me Faith! I cry.

Without some glimmering in my heart,
I could not raise this fervent prayer;
But, oh! a stronger light impart,
And in Thy mercy fix it there.

While Faith is with me, I am blest;
It turns my darkest night to day;
But while I clasp it to my breast,
I often feel it slide away.

Then, cold and dark, my spirit sinks,
To see my light of life depart;
And every fiend of Hell, methinks,
Enjoys the anguish of my heart.

What shall I do, if all my love,
My hopes, my toil, are cast away,
And if there be no God above,
To hear and bless me when I pray?

If this be vain delusion all,
If death be an eternal sleep,
And none can hear my secret call,
Or see the silent tears I weep!

Oh, help me, God! For thou alone
Canst my distracted soul relieve;
Forsake it not: it is thine own,
Though weak, yet longing to believe.

Oh, drive these cruel doubts away;
And make me know, that Thou art God!
A faith, that shines by night and day,
Will lighten every earthly load.

If I believe that Jesus died,
And waking, rose to reign above;
Then surely Sorrow, Sin, and Pride,
Must yield to Peace, and Hope, and Love.

And all the blessed words He said
Will strength and holy joy impart:
A shield of safety o'er my head,
A spring of comfort in my heart.

A WORD TO THE "ELECT"

You may rejoice to think *yourselves* secure;
You may be grateful for the gift divine—
That grace unsought, which made your black hearts pure,
And fits your earth-born souls in Heaven to shine.

But, is it sweet to look around, and view
Thousands excluded from that happiness
Which they deserved, at least, as much as you.—
Their faults not greater, nor their virtues less?

And wherefore should you love your God the more,
Because to you alone his smiles are given;
Because He chose to pass the *many* o'er,
And only bring the favoured *few* to Heaven?

And, wherefore should your hearts more grateful prove,
Because for *all* the Saviour did not die?
Is yours the God of justice and of love?
And are your bosoms warm with charity?

Say, does your heart expand to all mankind?
And, would you ever to your neighbour do—
The weak, the strong, the enlightened, and the blind—
As you would have your neighbour do to you?

And when you, looking on your fellow-men,
Behold them doomed to endless misery,
How can you talk of joy and rapture then?—
May God withhold such cruel joy from me!

That none deserve eternal bliss I know;
Unmerited the grace in mercy given:
But, none shall sink to everlasting woe,
That have not well deserved the wrath of Heaven.

And, oh! there lives within my heart
    A hope, long nursed by me;
(And should its cheering ray depart,
    How dark my soul would be!)

That as in Adam all have died,
    In Christ shall all men live;
And ever round his throne abide,
    Eternal praise to give.

That even the wicked shall at last
   Be fitted for the skies;
And when their dreadful doom is past,
   To life and light arise.

I ask not, how remote the day,
   Nor what the sinners' woe,
Before their dross is purged away;
   Enough for me to know—

That when the clip of wrath is drained,
   The metal purified,
They'll cling to what they once disdained,
   And live by Him that died.

PAST DAYS

'Tis strange to think there *was* a time
When mirth was not an empty name,
When laughter really cheered the heart,
And frequent smiles unbidden came,
And tears of grief would only flow
In sympathy for others' woe;

When speech expressed the inward thought,
And heart to kindred heart was bare,
And summer days were far too short
For all the pleasures crowded there;
And silence, solitude, and rest,
Now welcome to the weary breast—

Were all unprized, uncourted then—
And all the joy one spirit showed,
The other deeply felt again;
And friendship like a river flowed,
Constant and strong its silent course,
For nought withstood its gentle force:

When night, the holy time of peace,
Was dreaded as the parting hour;
When speech and mirth at once must cease,
And silence must resume her power;
Though ever free from pains and woes,
She only brought us calm repose.

And when the blessed dawn again
Brought daylight to the blushing skies,
We woke, and not *reluctant* then,
To joyless *labour* did we rise;
But full of hope, and glad and gay,
We welcomed the returning day.

THE CONSOLATION

Though bleak these woods, and damp the ground
   With fallen leaves so thickly strown,
And cold the wind that wanders round
   With wild and melancholy moan;

There *is* a friendly roof, I know,
   Might shield me from the wintry blast;
There is a fire, whose ruddy glow
   Will cheer me for my wanderings past.

And so, though still, where'er I go,
   Cold stranger-glances meet my eye;
Though, when my spirit sinks in woe,
   Unheeded swells the unbidden sigh;

Though solitude, endured too long,
   Bids youthful joys too soon decay,
Makes mirth a stranger to my tongue,
   And overclouds my noon of day;

When kindly thoughts that would have way,
   Flow back discouraged to my breast;
I know there is, though far away,
   A home where heart and soul may rest.

Warm hands are there, that, clasped in mine,
   The warmer heart will not belie;
While mirth, and truth, and friendship shine
   In smiling lip and earnest eye.

The ice that gathers round my heart
   May there be thawed; and sweetly, then,
The joys of youth, that now depart,
   Will come to cheer my soul again.

Though far I roam, that thought shall be
   My hope, my comfort, everywhere;
While such a home remains to me,
   My heart shall never know despair!

LINES COMPOSED IN A WOOD ON A WINDY DAY

My soul is awakened, my spirit is soaring
   And carried aloft on the wings of the breeze;
For above and around me the wild wind is roaring,
   Arousing to rapture the earth and the seas.

The long withered grass in the sunshine is glancing,
   The bare trees are tossing their branches on high;
The dead leaves beneath them are merrily dancing,
   The white clouds are scudding across the blue sky

I wish I could see how the ocean is lashing
   The foam of its billows to whirlwinds of spray;
I wish I could see how its proud waves are dashing,
   And hear the wild roar of their thunder to-day!

VIEWS OF LIFE

When sinks my heart in hopeless gloom,
And life can show no joy for me;
And I behold a yawning tomb,
Where bowers and palaces should be;

In vain you talk of morbid dreams;
In vain you gaily smiling say,
That what to me so dreary seems,
The healthy mind deems bright and gay.

I too have smiled, and thought like you,
But madly smiled, and falsely deemed:
Truth led me to the present view,—
I'm waking now—'twas *then* I dreamed.

I lately saw a sunset sky,
And stood enraptured to behold
Its varied hues of glorious dye:
First, fleecy clouds of shining gold;

These blushing took a rosy hue;
Beneath them shone a flood of green;
Nor less divine, the glorious blue
That smiled above them and between.

I cannot name each lovely shade;
I cannot say how bright they shone;
But one by one, I saw them fade;
And what remained when they were gone?

Dull clouds remained, of sombre hue,
And when their borrowed charm was o'er,
The azure sky had faded too,
That smiled so softly bright before.

So, gilded by the glow of youth,
Our varied life looks fair and gay;
And so remains the naked truth,
When that false light is past away.

Why blame ye, then, my keener sight,
That clearly sees a world of woes
Through all the haze of golden light
That flattering Falsehood round it throws?

When the young mother smiles above
The first-born darling of her heart,
Her bosom glows with earnest love,
While tears of silent transport start.

Fond dreamer! little does she know
The anxious toil, the suffering,
The blasted hopes, the burning woe,
The object of her joy will bring.

Her blinded eyes behold not now
What, soon or late, must be his doom;
The anguish that will cloud his brow,
The bed of death, the dreary tomb.

As little know the youthful pair,
In mutual love supremely blest,
What weariness, and cold despair,
Ere long, will seize the aching breast.

And even should Love and Faith remain,
(The greatest blessings life can show,)
Amid adversity and pain,
To shine throughout with cheering glow;

They do not see how cruel Death
Comes on, their loving hearts to part:
One feels not now the gasping breath,
The rending of the earth-bound heart,—

The soul's and body's agony,
Ere she may sink to her repose.
The sad survivor cannot see
The grave above his darling close;

Nor how, despairing and alone,
He then must wear his life away;
And linger, feebly toiling on,
And fainting, sink into decay.

      *   *   *   *

Oh, Youth may listen patiently,
While sad Experience tells her tale,
But Doubt sits smiling in his eye,
For ardent Hope will still prevail!

He hears how feeble Pleasure dies,
By guilt destroyed, and pain and woe;
He turns to Hope—and she replies,
"Believe it not-it is not so!"

"Oh, heed her not!" Experience says;
"For thus she whispered once to me;
She told me, in my youthful days,
How glorious manhood's prime would be.

"When, in the time of early Spring,
Too chill the winds that o'er me pass'd,
She said, each coming day would bring
A fairer heaven, a gentler blast.

"And when the sun too seldom beamed,
The sky, o'ercast, too darkly frowned,
The soaking rain too constant streamed,
And mists too dreary gathered round;

"She told me, Summer's glorious ray
Would chase those vapours all away,
   And scatter glories round;
With sweetest music fill the trees,
Load with rich scent the gentle breeze,
   And strew with flowers the ground

"But when, beneath that scorching ray,
I languished, weary through the day,
   While birds refused to sing,
Verdure decayed from field and tree,
And panting Nature mourned with me
   The freshness of the Spring.

"'Wait but a little while,' she said,
'Till Summer's burning days are fled;
   And Autumn shall restore,
With golden riches of her own,
And Summer's glories mellowed down,
   The freshness you deplore.'

And long I waited, but in vain:
That freshness never came again,
   Though Summer passed away,
Though Autumn's mists hung cold and chill.
And drooping nature languished still,
   And sank into decay.

"Till wintry blasts foreboding blew
Through leafless trees—and then I knew
   That Hope was all a dream.
But thus, fond youth, she cheated me;
And she will prove as false to thee,
   Though sweet her words may seem.

Stern prophet! Cease thy bodings dire—
Thou canst not quench the ardent fire
   That warms the breast of youth.
Oh, let it cheer him while it may,
And gently, gently die away—
   Chilled by the damps of truth!

Tell him, that earth is not our rest;
Its joys are empty—frail at best;
   And point beyond the sky.
But gleams of light may reach us here;
And hope the *roughest* path can cheer:
   Then do not bid it fly!

Though hope may promise joys, that still
Unkindly time will ne'er fulfil;
   Or, if they come at all,
We never find them unalloyed,—
Hurtful perchance, or soon destroyed,
   They vanish or they pall;

Yet hope *itself* a brightness throws
O'er all our labours and our woes;
   While dark foreboding Care
A thousand ills will oft portend,
That Providence may ne'er intend
   The trembling heart to bear.

Or if they come, it oft appears,
Our woes are lighter than our fears,
   And far more bravely borne.
Then let us not enhance our doom
But e'en in midnight's blackest gloom
   Expect the rising morn.

Because the road is rough and long,
Shall we despise the skylark's song,
   That cheers the wanderer's way?
Or trample down, with reckless feet,
The smiling flowerets, bright and sweet,
   Because they soon decay?

Pass pleasant scenes unnoticed by,
Because the next is bleak and drear;
Or not enjoy a smiling sky,
Because a tempest may be near?

No! while we journey on our way,
We'll smile on every lovely thing;
And ever, as they pass away,
To memory and hope we'll cling.

And though that awful river flows
Before us, when the journey's past,
Perchance of all the pilgrim's woes
Most dreadful—shrink not—'tis the last!

Though icy cold, and dark, and deep;
Beyond it smiles that blessed shore,
Where none shall suffer, none shall weep,
And bliss shall reign for evermore!

APPEAL

Oh, I am very weary,
   Though tears no longer flow;
My eyes are tired of weeping,
   My heart is sick of woe;

My life is very lonely
   My days pass heavily,
I'm weary of repining;
   Wilt thou not come to me?

Oh, didst thou know my longings
   For thee, from day to day,
My hopes, so often blighted,
   Thou wouldst not thus delay!

THE STUDENT'S SERENADE

I have slept upon my couch,
But my spirit did not rest,
For the labours of the day
Yet my weary soul opprest;

And before my dreaming eyes
Still the learned volumes lay,
And I could not close their leaves,
And I could not turn away.

But I oped my eyes at last,
And I heard a muffled sound;
'Twas the night-breeze, come to say
That the snow was on the ground.

Then I knew that there was rest
On the mountain's bosom free;
So I left my fevered couch,
And I flew to waken thee!

I have flown to waken thee—
For, if thou wilt not arise,
Then my soul can drink no peace
From these holy moonlight skies.

And this waste of virgin snow
To my sight will not be fair,
Unless thou wilt smiling come,
Love, to wander with me there.

Then, awake! Maria, wake!
For, if thou couldst only know
How the quiet moonlight sleeps
On this wilderness of snow,

And the groves of ancient trees,
In their snowy garb arrayed,
Till they stretch into the gloom
Of the distant valley's shade;

I know thou wouldst rejoice
To inhale this bracing air;
Thou wouldst break thy sweetest sleep
To behold a scene so fair.

O'er these wintry wilds, *alone*,
Thou wouldst joy to wander free;
And it will not please thee less,
Though that bliss be shared with me.

THE CAPTIVE DOVE

Poor restless dove, I pity thee;
And when I hear thy plaintive moan,
I mourn for thy captivity,
And in thy woes forget mine own.

To see thee stand prepared to fly,
And flap those useless wings of thine,
And gaze into the distant sky,
Would melt a harder heart than mine.

In vain—in vain! Thou canst not rise:
Thy prison roof confines thee there;
Its slender wires delude thine eyes,
And quench thy longings with despair.

Oh, thou wert made to wander free
In sunny mead and shady grove,
And far beyond the rolling sea,
In distant climes, at will to rove!

Yet, hadst thou but one gentle mate
Thy little drooping heart to cheer,
And share with thee thy captive state,
Thou couldst be happy even there.

Yes, even there, if, listening by,
One faithful dear companion stood,
While gazing on her full bright eye,
Thou mightst forget thy native wood

But thou, poor solitary dove,
Must make, unheard, thy joyless moan;
The heart that Nature formed to love
Must pine, neglected, and alone.

SELF-CONGRATULATION

Ellen, you were thoughtless once
    Of beauty or of grace,
Simple and homely in attire,
    Careless of form and face;
Then whence this change? and wherefore now
    So often smoothe your hair?
And wherefore deck your youthful form
    With such unwearied care?

Tell us, and cease to tire our ears
    With that familiar strain;
Why will you play those simple tunes
    So often o'er again?
"Indeed, dear friends, I can but say
    That childhood's thoughts are gone;
Each year its own new feelings brings,
    And years move swiftly on:

"And for these little simple airs—
    I love to play them o'er
So much—I dare not promise, now,
    To play them never more."
I answered—and it was enough;
    They turned them to depart;
They could not read my secret thoughts,
    Nor see my throbbing heart.

I've noticed many a youthful form,
    Upon whose changeful face
The inmost workings of the soul
    The gazer well might trace;
The speaking eye, the changing lip,
    The ready blushing cheek,
The smiling, or beclouded brow,
    Their different feelings speak.

But, thank God! you might gaze on mine
    For hours, and never know
The secret changes of my soul
    From joy to keenest woe.
Last night, as we sat round the fire
    Conversing merrily,
We heard, without, approaching steps
    Of one well known to me!

There was no trembling in my voice,
    No blush upon my cheek,
No lustrous sparkle in my eyes,
    Of hope, or joy, to speak;
But, oh! my spirit burned within,
    My heart beat full and fast!
He came not nigh—he went away—
    And then my joy was past.

And yet my comrades marked it not:
    My voice was still the same;
They saw me smile, and o'er my face
    No signs of sadness came.
They little knew my hidden thoughts;
    And they will *never* know
The aching anguish of my heart,
    The bitter burning woe!

FLUCTUATIONS

What though the Sun had left my sky;
   To save me from despair
The blessed Moon arose on high,
   And shone serenely there.

I watched her, with a tearful gaze,
   Rise slowly o'er the hill,
While through the dim horizon's haze
   Her light gleamed faint and chill.

I thought such wan and lifeless beams
   Could ne'er my heart repay
For the bright sun's most transient gleams
   That cheered me through the day:

But, as above that mist's control
   She rose, and brighter shone,
I felt her light upon my soul;
   But now—that light is gone!

Thick vapours snatched her from my sight,
   And I was darkling left,
All in the cold and gloomy night,
   Of light and hope bereft:

Until, methought, a little star
   Shone forth with trembling ray,
To cheer me with its light afar—
   But that, too, passed away.

Anon, an earthly meteor blazed
   The gloomy darkness through;
I smiled, yet trembled while I gazed—
   But that soon vanished too!

And darker, drearier fell the night
   Upon my spirit then;—
But what is that faint struggling light?
   Is it the Moon again?

Kind Heaven! increase that silvery gleam
   And bid these clouds depart,
And let her soft celestial beam
   Restore my fainting heart!

SELECTIONS FROM THE LITERARY REMAINS OF ELLIS AND ACTON BELL.

BY CURRER BELL

SELECTIONS FROM POEMS BY ELLIS BELL

It would not have been difficult to compile a volume out of the papers left by my sisters, had I, in making the selection, dismissed from my consideration the scruples and the wishes of those whose written thoughts these papers held. But this was impossible: an influence, stronger than could be exercised by any motive of expediency, necessarily regulated the selection. I have, then, culled from the mass only a little poem here and there. The whole makes but a tiny nosegay, and the colour and perfume of the flowers are not such as fit them for festal uses.

It has been already said that my sisters wrote much in childhood and girlhood. Usually, it seems a sort of injustice to expose in print the crude thoughts of the unripe mind, the rude efforts of the unpractised hand; yet I venture to give three little poems of my sister Emily's, written in her sixteenth year, because they illustrate a point in her character.

At that period she was sent to school. Her previous life, with the exception of a single half-year, had been passed in the absolute retirement of a village parsonage, amongst the hills bordering Yorkshire and Lancashire. The scenery of these hills is not grand—it is not romantic it is scarcely striking. Long low moors, dark with heath, shut in little valleys, where a stream waters, here and there, a fringe of stunted copse. Mills and scattered cottages chase romance from these valleys; it is only higher up, deep in amongst the ridges of the moors, that Imagination can find rest for the sole of her foot: and even if she finds it there, she must be a solitude-loving raven—no gentle dove. If she demand beauty to inspire her, she must bring it inborn: these moors are too stern to yield any product so delicate. The eye of the gazer must *itself* brim with a "purple light," intense enough to perpetuate the brief flower-flush of August on the heather, or the rare sunset-smile of June; out of his heart must well the freshness, that in latter spring and early summer brightens the bracken, nurtures the moss, and cherishes the starry flowers that spangle for a few weeks the pasture of the moor-sheep. Unless that light and freshness are innate and self-sustained, the drear prospect of a Yorkshire moor will be found as barren of poetic as of agricultural interest: where the love of wild nature is strong, the locality will perhaps be clung to with the more passionate constancy, because from the hill-lover's self comes half its charm.

My sister Emily loved the moors. Flowers brighter than the rose bloomed in the blackest of the heath for her; out of a sullen hollow in a livid hill-side her mind could make an Eden. She found in the bleak solitude many and dear delights; and not the least and best loved was—liberty.

Liberty was the breath of Emily's nostrils; without it, she perished. The change from her own home to a school, and from her own very noiseless, very secluded, but unrestricted and inartificial mode of life, to one of disciplined routine (though under the kindliest auspices), was what she failed in enduring. Her nature proved here too strong for her fortitude. Every morning when she woke, the vision of home and the moors rushed on her, and darkened and saddened the day that lay before her. Nobody knew what ailed her but me—I knew only too well. In this struggle her health was quickly broken: her white face, attenuated form, and failing strength, threatened rapid decline. I felt in my heart she would die, if she did not go home, and with this conviction obtained her recall. She had only been three months at school; and it was some years before the experiment of sending her from home was again ventured on. After the age of twenty, having meantime studied alone with diligence and perseverance, she went with me to an establishment on the Continent: the same suffering and conflict ensued, heightened by the strong recoil of her upright, heretic and English spirit from the gentle Jesuitry of the foreign and Romish system. Once more she seemed sinking, but this time she rallied through the mere force of resolution: with inward remorse and shame she looked back on her former failure, and resolved to conquer in this second ordeal. She did conquer: but the victory cost her dear. She was never happy till she carried her hard-won knowledge back to the remote English village, the old parsonage-house, and desolate Yorkshire hills. A very few years more, and she looked her last on those hills, and breathed her last in that house, and under the aisle of that obscure village church found her last lowly resting-place. Merciful was the decree that spared her when she was a stranger in a strange land, and guarded her dying bed with kindred love and congenial constancy.

The following pieces were composed at twilight, in the school-room, when the leisure of the evening play-hour brought back in full tide the thoughts of home.

I

A little while, a little while,
   The weary task is put away,
And I can sing and I can smile,
   Alike, while I have holiday.

Where wilt thou go, my harassed heart—
   What thought, what scene invites thee now
What spot, or near or far apart,
   Has rest for thee, my weary brow?

There is a spot, 'mid barren hills,
   Where winter howls, and driving rain;
But, if the dreary tempest chills,
   There is a light that warms again.

The house is old, the trees are bare,
   Moonless above bends twilight's dome;
But what on earth is half so dear—
   So longed for—as the hearth of home?

The mute bird sitting on the stone,
   The dank moss dripping from the wall,
The thorn-trees gaunt, the walks o'ergrown,
   I love them—how I love them all!

Still, as I mused, the naked room,
  The alien firelight died away;
And from the midst of cheerless gloom,
  I passed to bright, unclouded day.

A little and a lone green lane
  That opened on a common wide;
A distant, dreamy, dim blue chain
  Of mountains circling every side.

A heaven so clear, an earth so calm,
  So sweet, so soft, so hushed an air;
And, deepening still the dream-like charm,
  Wild moor-sheep feeding everywhere.

That was the scene, I knew it well;
  I knew the turfy pathway's sweep,
That, winding o'er each billowy swell,
  Marked out the tracks of wandering sheep.

Could I have lingered but an hour,
  It well had paid a week of toil;
But Truth has banished Fancy's power:
  Restraint and heavy task recoil.

Even as I stood with raptured eye,
  Absorbed in bliss so deep and dear,
My hour of rest had fleeted by,
  And back came labour, bondage, care.

II

THE BLUEBELL

The Bluebell is the sweetest flower
  That waves in summer air:
Its blossoms have the mightiest power
  To soothe my spirit's care.

There is a spell in purple heath
  Too wildly, sadly dear;
The violet has a fragrant breath,
  But fragrance will not cheer,

The trees are bare, the sun is cold,
    And seldom, seldom seen;
The heavens have lost their zone of gold,
    And earth her robe of green.

And ice upon the glancing stream
    Has cast its sombre shade;
And distant hills and valleys seem
    In frozen mist arrayed.

The Bluebell cannot charm me now,
    The heath has lost its bloom;
The violets in the glen below,
    They yield no sweet perfume.

But, though I mourn the sweet Bluebell,
    'Tis better far away;
I know how fast my tears would swell
    To see it smile to-day.

For, oh! when chill the sunbeams fall
    Adown that dreary sky,
And gild yon dank and darkened wall
    With transient brilliancy;

How do I weep, how do I pine
    For the time of flowers to come,
And turn me from that fading shine,
    To mourn the fields of home!

III

Loud without the wind was roaring
    Through th' autumnal sky;
Drenching wet, the cold rain pouring,
    Spoke of winter nigh.
        All too like that dreary eve,
        Did my exiled spirit grieve.
Grieved at first, but grieved not long,
    Sweet—how softly sweet!—it came;
Wild words of an ancient song,
    Undefined, without a name.

"It was spring, and the skylark was singing:"
    Those words they awakened a spell;
They unlocked a deep fountain, whose springing,
    Nor absence, nor distance can quell.

In the gloom of a cloudy November
   They uttered the music of May;
They kindled the perishing ember
   Into fervour that could not decay.

Awaken, o'er all my dear moorland,
   West-wind, in thy glory and pride!
Oh! call me from valley and lowland,
   To walk by the hill-torrent's side!

It is swelled with the first snowy weather;
   The rocks they are icy and hoar,
And sullenly waves the long heather,
   And the fern leaves are sunny no more.

There are no yellow stars on the mountain
   The bluebells have long died away
From the brink of the moss-bedded fountain—
   From the side of the wintry brae.

But lovelier than corn-fields all waving
   In emerald, and vermeil, and gold,
Are the heights where the north-wind is raving,
   And the crags where I wandered of old.

It was morning: the bright sun was beaming;
   How sweetly it brought back to me
The time when nor labour nor dreaming
   Broke the sleep of the happy and free!

But blithely we rose as the dawn-heaven
   Was melting to amber and blue,
And swift were the wings to our feet given,
   As we traversed the meadows of dew.

For the moors! For the moors, where the short grass
   Like velvet beneath us should lie!
For the moors! For the moors, where each high pass
   Rose sunny against the clear sky!

For the moors, where the linnet was trilling
   Its song on the old granite stone;
Where the lark, the wild sky-lark, was filling
   Every breast with delight like its own!

What language can utter the feeling
   Which rose, when in exile afar,
On the brow of a lonely hill kneeling,
   I saw the brown heath growing there?

It was scattered and stunted, and told me
   That soon even that would be gone:
It whispered, "The grim walls enfold me,
   I have bloomed in my last summer's sun."

But not the loved music, whose waking
   Makes the soul of the Swiss die away,
Has a spell more adored and heartbreaking
   Than for me, in that blighted heath lay.

The spirit which bent 'neath its power,
   How it longed—how it burned to be free!
If I could have wept in that hour,
   Those tears had been heaven to me.

Well—well; the sad minutes are moving,
   Though loaded with trouble and pain;
And some time the loved and the loving
   Shall meet on the mountains again!

The following little piece has no title; but in it the Genius of a solitary region seems to address his wandering and wayward votary, and to recall within his influence the proud mind which rebelled at times even against what it most loved.

Shall earth no more inspire thee,
   Thou lonely dreamer now?
Since passion may not fire thee,
   Shall nature cease to bow?

Thy mind is ever moving,
   In regions dark to thee;
Recall its useless roving,
   Come back, and dwell with me.

I know my mountain breezes
   Enchant and soothe thee still,
I know my sunshine pleases,
   Despite thy wayward will.

When day with evening blending,
   Sinks from the summer sky,
I've seen thy spirit bending
   In fond idolatry.

I've watched thee every hour;
   I know my mighty sway:
I know my magic power
   To drive thy griefs away.

Few hearts to mortals given,
   On earth so wildly pine;
Yet few would ask a heaven
   More like this earth than thine.

Then let my winds caress thee
   Thy comrade let me be:
Since nought beside can bless thee,
   Return—and dwell with me.

Here again is the same mind in converse with a like abstraction. "The Night-Wind," breathing through an open window, has visited an ear which discerned language in its whispers.

THE NIGHT-WIND

In summer's mellow midnight,
   A cloudless moon shone through
Our open parlour window,
   And rose-trees wet with dew.

I sat in silent musing;
   The soft wind waved my hair;
It told me heaven was glorious,
   And sleeping earth was fair.

I needed not its breathing
   To bring such thoughts to me;
But still it whispered lowly,
   How dark the woods will be!

"The thick leaves in my murmur
   Are rustling like a dream,
And all their myriad voices
   Instinct with spirit seem."

I said, "Go, gentle singer,
  Thy wooing voice is kind:
But do not think its music
  Has power to reach my mind.

"Play with the scented flower,
  The young tree's supple bough,
And leave my human feelings
  In their own course to flow."

The wanderer would not heed me;
  Its kiss grew warmer still.
"O come!" it sighed so sweetly;
  "I'll win thee 'gainst thy will.

"Were we not friends from childhood?
  Have I not loved thee long?
As long as thou, the solemn night,
  Whose silence wakes my song.

"And when thy heart is resting
  Beneath the church-aisle stone,
I shall have time for mourning,
  And *thou* for being alone."

In these stanzas a louder gale has roused the sleeper on her pillow: the wakened soul struggles to blend with the storm by which it is stayed:—

Aye—there it is! it wakes to-night
  Deep feelings I thought dead;
Strong in the blast—quick gathering light—
  The heart's flame kindles red.

"Now I can tell by thine altered cheek,
  And by thine eyes' full gaze,
And by the words thou scarce dost speak,
  How wildly fancy plays.

"Yes—I could swear that glorious wind
  Has swept the world aside,
Has dashed its memory from thy mind
  Like foam-bells from the tide:

"And thou art now a spirit pouring
  Thy presence into all:
The thunder of the tempest's roaring,
  The whisper of its fall:

"An universal influence,
  From thine own influence free;
A principle of life—intense—
  Lost to mortality.

"Thus truly, when that breast is cold,
  Thy prisoned soul shall rise;
The dungeon mingle with the mould—
The captive with the skies.
  Nature's deep being, thine shall hold,
Her spirit all thy spirit fold,
  Her breath absorb thy sighs.
Mortal! though soon life's tale is told;
  Who once lives, never dies!"

LOVE AND FRIENDSHIP

Love is like the wild rose-briar;
  Friendship like the holly-tree.
The holly is dark when the rose-briar blooms,
  But which will bloom most constantly?

The wild rose-briar is sweet in spring,
  Its summer blossoms scent the air;
Yet wait till winter comes again,
  And who will call the wild-briar fair?

Then, scorn the silly rose-wreath now,
  And deck thee with the holly's sheen,
That, when December blights thy brow,
  He still may leave thy garland green.

THE ELDER'S REBUKE

"Listen! When your hair, like mine,
Takes a tint of silver gray;
When your eyes, with dimmer shine,
Watch life's bubbles float away:

When you, young man, have borne like me
The weary weight of sixty-three,
Then shall penance sore be paid
  For those hours so wildly squandered;
And the words that now fall dead
  On your ear, be deeply pondered—
Pondered and approved at last:
But their virtue will be past!

"Glorious is the prize of Duty,
   Though she be 'a serious power';
Treacherous all the lures of Beauty,
   Thorny bud and poisonous flower!

"Mirth is but a mad beguiling
   Of the golden-gifted time;
Love—a demon-meteor, wiling
   Heedless feet to gulfs of crime.

"Those who follow earthly pleasure,
   Heavenly knowledge will not lead;
Wisdom hides from them her treasure,
   Virtue bids them evil-speed!

"Vainly may their hearts repenting.
   Seek for aid in future years;
Wisdom, scorned, knows no relenting;
   Virtue is not won by fears."

Thus spake the ice-blooded elder gray;
The young man scoffed as he turned away,
Turned to the call of a sweet lute's measure,
Waked by the lightsome touch of pleasure:
Had he ne'er met a gentler teacher,
Woe had been wrought by that pitiless preacher.

THE WANDERER FROM THE FOLD

How few, of all the hearts that loved,
   Are grieving for thee now;
And why should mine to-night be moved
   With such a sense of woe?

Too often thus, when left alone,
   Where none my thoughts can see,
Comes back a word, a passing tone
   From thy strange history.

Sometimes I seem to see thee rise,
   A glorious child again;
All virtues beaming from thine eyes
   That ever honoured men:

Courage and truth, a generous breast
   Where sinless sunshine lay:
A being whose very presence blest
   Like gladsome summer-day.

O, fairly spread thy early sail,
   And fresh, and pure, and free,
Was the first impulse of the gale
   Which urged life's wave for thee!

Why did the pilot, too confiding,
   Dream o'er that ocean's foam,
And trust in Pleasure's careless guiding
   To bring his vessel home?

For well he knew what dangers frowned,
   What mists would gather, dim;
What rocks and shelves, and sands lay round
   Between his port and him.

The very brightness of the sun
   The splendour of the main,
The wind which bore him wildly on
   Should not have warned in vain.

An anxious gazer from the shore—
   I marked the whitening wave,
And wept above thy fate the more
   Because—I could not save.

It recks not now, when all is over:
   But yet my heart will be
A mourner still, though friend and lover
   Have both forgotten thee!

WARNING AND REPLY

In the earth—the earth—thou shalt be laid,
   A grey stone standing over thee;
Black mould beneath thee spread,
   And black mould to cover thee.

"Well—there is rest there,
   So fast come thy prophecy;
The time when my sunny hair
   Shall with grass roots entwined be."

But cold—cold is that resting-place,
   Shut out from joy and liberty,
And all who loved thy living face
   Will shrink from it shudderingly,

"Not so. *Here* the world is chill,
   And sworn friends fall from me:
But *there*—they will own me still,
   And prize my memory."

Farewell, then, all that love,
   All that deep sympathy:
Sleep on: Heaven laughs above,
   Earth never misses thee.

Turf-sod and tombstone drear
   Part human company;
One heart breaks only—here,
   But that heart was worthy thee!

LAST WORDS

I knew not 'twas so dire a crime
   To say the word, "Adieu;"
But this shall be the only time
   My lips or heart shall sue.

That wild hill-side, the winter morn,
   The gnarled and ancient tree,
If in your breast they waken scorn,
   Shall wake the same in me.

I can forget black eyes and brows,
   And lips of falsest charm,
If you forget the sacred vows
   Those faithless lips could form.

If hard commands can tame your love,
   Or strongest walls can hold,
I would not wish to grieve above
   A thing so false and cold.

And there are bosoms bound to mine
   With links both tried and strong:
And there are eyes whose lightning shine
   Has warmed and blest me long:

Those eyes shall make my only day,
    Shall set my spirit free,
And chase the foolish thoughts away
    That mourn your memory.

THE LADY TO HER GUITAR

For him who struck thy foreign string,
    I ween this heart has ceased to care;
Then why dost thou such feelings bring
    To my sad spirit—old Guitar?

It is as if the warm sunlight
    In some deep glen should lingering stay,
When clouds of storm, or shades of night,
    Have wrapt the parent orb away.

It is as if the glassy brook
    Should image still its willows fair,
Though years ago the woodman's stroke
    Laid low in dust their Dryad-hair.

Even so, Guitar, thy magic tone
    Hath moved the tear and waked the sigh:
Hath bid the ancient torrent moan,
    Although its very source is dry.

THE TWO CHILDREN

Heavy hangs the rain-drop
    From the burdened spray;
Heavy broods the damp mist
    On uplands far away.

Heavy looms the dull sky,
    Heavy rolls the sea;
And heavy throbs the young heart
    Beneath that lonely tree.

Never has a blue streak
    Cleft the clouds since morn;
Never has his grim fate
    Smiled since he was born.

Frowning on the infant,
  Shadowing childhood's joy
Guardian-angel knows not
  That melancholy boy.

Day is passing swiftly
  Its sad and sombre prime;
Boyhood sad is merging
  In sadder manhood's time:

All the flowers are praying
  For sun, before they close,
And he prays too—unconscious—
  That sunless human rose.

Blossom—that the west-wind
  Has never wooed to blow,
Scentless are thy petals,
  Thy dew is cold as snow!

Soul—where kindred kindness,
  No early promise woke,
Barren is thy beauty,
  As weed upon a rock.

Wither—soul and blossom!
  You both were vainly given;
Earth reserves no blessing
  For the unblest of heaven!

Child of delight, with sun-bright hair,
  And sea-blue, sea-deep eyes!
Spirit of bliss! What brings thee here
  Beneath these sullen skies?

Thou shouldst live in eternal spring,
  Where endless day is never dim;
Why, Seraph, has thine erring wing
  Wafted thee down to weep with him?

"Ah! not from heaven am I descended,
  Nor do I come to mingle tears;
But sweet is day, though with shadows blended;
  And, though clouded, sweet are youthful years.

"I—the image of light and gladness—
   Saw and pitied that mournful boy,
And I vowed—if need were—to share his sadness,
   And give to him my sunny joy.

"Heavy and dark the night is closing;
   Heavy and dark may its biding be:
Better for all from grief reposing,
   And better for all who watch like me—

"Watch in love by a fevered pillow,
   Cooling the fever with pity's balm
Safe as the petrel on tossing billow,
   Safe in mine own soul's golden calm!

"Guardian-angel he lacks no longer;
   Evil fortune he need not fear:
Fate is strong, but love is stronger;
   And *my* love is truer than angel-care."

THE VISIONARY

Silent is the house: all are laid asleep:
One alone looks out o'er the snow-wreaths deep,
Watching every cloud, dreading every breeze
That whirls the wildering drift, and bends the groaning trees.

Cheerful is the hearth, soft the matted floor;
Not one shivering gust creeps through pane or door;
The little lamp burns straight, its rays shoot strong and far:
I trim it well, to be the wanderer's guiding-star.

Frown, my haughty sire! chide, my angry dame!
Set your slaves to spy; threaten me with shame:
But neither sire nor dame, nor prying serf shall know,
What angel nightly tracks that waste of frozen snow.

What I love shall come like visitant of air,
Safe in secret power from lurking human snare;
What loves me, no word of mine shall e'er betray,
Though for faith unstained my life must forfeit pay

Burn, then, little lamp; glimmer straight and clear—
Hush! a rustling wing stirs, methinks, the air:
He for whom I wait, thus ever comes to me;
Strange Power! I trust thy might; trust thou my constancy.

ENCOURAGEMENT

I do not weep; I would not weep;
  Our mother needs no tears:
Dry thine eyes, too; 'tis vain to keep
  This causeless grief for years.

What though her brow be changed and cold,
  Her sweet eyes closed for ever?
What though the stone—the darksome mould
  Our mortal bodies sever?

What though her hand smooth ne'er again
  Those silken locks of thine?
Nor, through long hours of future pain,
  Her kind face o'er thee shine?

Remember still, she is not dead;
  She sees us, sister, now;
Laid, where her angel spirit fled,
  'Mid heath and frozen snow.

And from that world of heavenly light
  Will she not always bend
To guide us in our lifetime's night,
  And guard us to the end?

Thou knowest she will; and thou mayst mourn
  That *we* are left below:
But not that she can ne'er return
  To share our earthly woe.

STANZAS

Often rebuked, yet always back returning
  To those first feelings that were born with me,
And leaving busy chase of wealth and learning
  For idle dreams of things which cannot be:

To-day, I will seek not the shadowy region;
  Its unsustaining vastness waxes drear;
And visions rising, legion after legion,
  Bring the unreal world too strangely near.

I'll walk, but not in old heroic traces,
   And not in paths of high morality,
And not among the half-distinguished faces,
   The clouded forms of long-past history.

I'll walk where my own nature would be leading:
   It vexes me to choose another guide:
Where the grey flocks in ferny glens are feeding;
   Where the wild wind blows on the mountain side.

What have those lonely mountains worth revealing?
   More glory and more grief than I can tell:
The earth that wakes *one* human heart to feeling
   Can centre both the worlds of Heaven and Hell.

The following are the last lines my sister Emily ever wrote:—

   No coward soul is mine,
No trembler in the world's storm-troubled sphere:
   I see Heaven's glories shine,
And faith shines equal, arming me from fear.

   O God within my breast,
Almighty, ever-present Deity!
   Life—that in me has rest,
As I—undying Life—have power in thee!

   Vain are the thousand creeds
That move men's hearts: unutterably vain;
   Worthless as withered weeds,
Or idlest froth amid the boundless main,

   To waken doubt in one
Holding so fast by thine infinity;
   So surely anchored on
The stedfast rock of immortality.

   With wide-embracing love
Thy spirit animates eternal years,
   Pervades and broods above,
Changes, sustains, dissolves, creates, and rears.

   Though earth and man were gone,
And suns and universes ceased to be,
   And Thou were left alone,
Every existence would exist in Thee.

There is not room for Death,
Nor atom that his might could render void:
Thou—*thou* art Being and Breath,
And what *thou* art may never be destroyed.

SELECTIONS FROM POEMS BY ACTON BELL

In looking over my sister Anne's papers, I find mournful evidence that religious feeling had been to her but too much like what it was to Cowper; I mean, of course, in a far milder form. Without rendering her a prey to those horrors that defy concealment, it subdued her mood and bearing to a perpetual pensiveness; the pillar of a cloud glided constantly before her eyes; she ever waited at the foot of a secret Sinai, listening in her heart to the voice of a trumpet sounding long and waxing louder. Some, perhaps, would rejoice over these tokens of sincere though sorrowing piety in a deceased relative: I own, to me they seem sad, as if her whole innocent life had been passed under the martyrdom of an unconfessed physical pain: their effect, indeed, would be too distressing, were it not combated by the certain knowledge that in her last moments this tyranny of a too tender conscience was overcome; this pomp of terrors broke up, and passing away, left her dying hour unclouded. Her belief in God did not then bring to her dread, as of a stern Judge,—but hope, as in a Creator and Saviour: and no faltering hope was it, but a sure and stedfast conviction, on which, in the rude passage from Time to Eternity, she threw the weight of her human weakness, and by which she was enabled to bear what was to be borne, patiently—serenely—victoriously.

DESPONDENCY

I have gone backward in the work;
　The labour has not sped;
Drowsy and dark my spirit lies,
　Heavy and dull as lead.

How can I rouse my sinking soul
　From such a lethargy?
How can I break these iron chains
　And set my spirit free?

There have been times when I have mourned!
　In anguish o'er the past,
And raised my suppliant hands on high,
　While tears fell thick and fast;

And prayed to have my sins forgiven,
　With such a fervent zeal,
An earnest grief, a strong desire
　As now I cannot feel.

And I have felt so full of love,
   So strong in spirit then,
As if my heart would never cool,
   Or wander back again.

And yet, alas! how many times
   My feet have gone astray!
How oft have I forgot my God!
   How greatly fallen away!

My sins increase—my love grows cold,
   And Hope within me dies:
Even Faith itself is wavering now;
   Oh, how shall I arise?

I cannot weep, but I can pray,
   Then let me not despair:
Lord Jesus, save me, lest I die!
   Christ, hear my humble prayer!

A PRAYER

My God (oh, let me call Thee mine,
   Weak, wretched sinner though I be),
My trembling soul would fain be Thine;
   My feeble faith still clings to Thee.

Not only for the Past I grieve,
   The Future fills me with dismay;
Unless Thou hasten to relieve,
   Thy suppliant is a castaway.

I cannot say my faith is strong,
   I dare not hope my love is great;
But strength and love to Thee belong;
   Oh, do not leave me desolate!

I know I owe my all to Thee;
   Oh, *take* the heart I cannot give!
Do Thou my strength—my Saviour be,
   And *make* me to Thy glory live.

IN MEMORY OF A HAPPY DAY IN FEBRUARY

Blessed be Thou for all the joy
  My soul has felt to-day!
Oh, let its memory stay with me,
  And never pass away!

I was alone, for those I loved
  Were far away from me;
The sun shone on the withered grass,
  The wind blew fresh and free.

Was it the smile of early spring
  That made my bosom glow?
'Twas sweet; but neither sun nor wind
  Could cheer my spirit so.

Was it some feeling of delight
  All vague and undefined?
No; 'twas a rapture deep and strong,
  Expanding in the mind.

Was it a sanguine view of life,
  And all its transient bliss,
A hope of bright prosperity?
  Oh, no! it was not this.

It was a glimpse of truth divine
  Unto my spirit given,
Illumined by a ray of light
  That shone direct from heaven.

I felt there was a God on high,
  By whom all things were made;
I saw His wisdom and His power
  In all his works displayed.

But most throughout the moral world,
  I saw his glory shine;
I saw His wisdom infinite,
  His mercy all divine.

Deep secrets of His providence,
  In darkness long concealed,
Unto the vision of my soul
  Were graciously revealed.

But while I wondered and adored
   His Majesty divine,
I did not tremble at His power:
   I felt that God was mine;

I knew that my Redeemer lived;
   I did not fear to die;
Full sure that I should rise again
   To immortality.

I longed to view that bliss divine,
   Which eye hath never seen;
Like Moses, I would see His face
   Without the veil between.

CONFIDENCE

Oppressed with sin and woe,
   A burdened heart I bear,
Opposed by many a mighty foe;
   But I will not despair.

With this polluted heart,
   I dare to come to Thee,
Holy and mighty as Thou art,
   For Thou wilt pardon me.

I feel that I am weak,
   And prone to every sin;
But Thou who giv'st to those who seek,
   Wilt give me strength within.

Far as this earth may be
   From yonder starry skies;
Remoter still am I from Thee:
   Yet Thou wilt not despise.

I need not fear my foes,
   I deed not yield to care;
I need not sink beneath my woes,
   For Thou wilt answer prayer.

In my Redeemer's name,
   I give myself to Thee;
And, all unworthy as I am,
   My God will cherish me.

My sister Anne had to taste the cup of life as it is mixed for the class termed "Governesses."
The following are some of the thoughts that now and then solace a governess:—

LINES WRITTEN FROM HOME

Though bleak these woods, and damp the ground,
    With fallen leaves so thickly strewn,
And cold the wind that wanders round
    With wild and melancholy moan;

There is a friendly roof I know,
    Might shield me from the wintry blast;
There is a fire whose ruddy glow
    Will cheer me for my wanderings past.

And so, though still where'er I go
    Cold stranger glances meet my eye;
Though, when my spirit sinks in woe,
    Unheeded swells the unbidden sigh;

Though solitude, endured too long,
    Bids youthful joys too soon decay,
Makes mirth a stranger to my tongue,
    And overclouds my noon of day;

When kindly thoughts that would have way
    Flow back, discouraged, to my breast,
I know there is, though far away,
    A home where heart and soul may rest.

Warm hands are there, that, clasped in mine,
    The warmer heart will not belie;
While mirth and truth, and friendship shine
    In smiling lip and earnest eye.

The ice that gathers round my heart
    May there be thawed; and sweetly, then,
The joys of youth, that now depart,
    Will come to cheer my soul again.

Though far I roam, that thought shall be
    My hope, my comfort everywhere;
While such a home remains to me,
    My heart shall never know despair.

THE NARROW WAY

Believe not those who say
   The upward path is smooth,
Lest thou shouldst stumble in the way,
   And faint before the truth.

It is the only road
   Unto the realms of joy;
But he who seeks that blest abode
   Must all his powers employ.

Bright hopes and pure delight
   Upon his course may beam,
And there, amid the sternest heights,
   The sweetest flowerets gleam.

On all her breezes borne,
   Earth yields no scents like those;
But he that dares not gasp the thorn
   Should never crave the rose.

Arm—arm thee for the fight!
   Cast useless loads away;
Watch through the darkest hours of night;
   Toil through the hottest day.

Crush pride into the dust,
   Or thou must needs be slack;
And trample down rebellious lust,
   Or it will hold thee back.

Seek not thy honour here;
   Waive pleasure and renown;
The world's dread scoff undaunted bear,
   And face its deadliest frown.

To labour and to love,
   To pardon and endure,
To lift thy heart to God above,
   And keep thy conscience pure;

Be this thy constant aim,
   Thy hope, thy chief delight;
What matter who should whisper blame
   Or who should scorn or slight?

What matter, if thy God approve,
  And if, within thy breast,
Thou feel the comfort of His love,
  The earnest of His rest?

DOMESTIC PEACE

Why should such gloomy silence reign,
  And why is all the house so drear,
When neither danger, sickness, pain,
  Nor death, nor want, have entered here?

We are as many as we were
  That other night, when all were gay
And full of hope, and free from care;
  Yet is there something gone away.

The moon without, as pure and calm,
  Is shining as that night she shone;
But now, to us, she brings no balm,
  For something from our hearts is gone.

Something whose absence leaves a void—
  A cheerless want in every heart;
Each feels the bliss of all destroyed,
  And mourns the change—but each apart.

The fire is burning in the grate
  As redly as it used to burn;
But still the hearth is desolate,
  Till mirth, and love, and *peace* return.

'Twas *peace* that flowed from heart to heart,
  With looks and smiles that spoke of heaven,
And gave us language to impart
  The blissful thoughts itself had given.

Domestic peace! best joy of earth,
  When shall we all thy value learn?
White angel, to our sorrowing hearth,
  Return—oh, graciously return!

THE THREE GUIDES[1]

Spirit of Earth! thy hand is chill:
   I've felt its icy clasp;
And, shuddering, I remember still
   That stony-hearted grasp.
Thine eye bids love and joy depart:
   Oh, turn its gaze from me!
It presses down my shrinking heart;
   I will not walk with thee!

"Wisdom is mine," I've heard thee say:
   "Beneath my searching eye
All mist and darkness melt away,
   Phantoms and fables fly.
Before me truth can stand alone,
   The naked, solid truth;
And man matured by worth will own,
   If I am shunned by youth.

"Firm is my tread, and sure though slow;
   My footsteps never slide;
And he that follows me shall know
   I am the surest guide."
Thy boast is vain; but were it true
   That thou couldst safely steer
Life's rough and devious pathway through,
   Such guidance I should fear.

How could I bear to walk for aye,
   With eyes to earthward prone,
O'er trampled weeds and miry clay,
   And sand and flinty stone;
Never the glorious view to greet
   Of hill and dale, and sky;
To see that Nature's charms are sweet,
   Or feel that Heaven is nigh?

---

[1] First published in *Fraser's Magazine*.

If in my heart arose a spring,
   A gush of thought divine,
At once stagnation thou wouldst bring
   With that cold touch of thine.
If, glancing up, I sought to snatch
   But one glimpse of the sky,
My baffled gaze would only catch
   Thy heartless, cold grey eye.

If to the breezes wandering near,
   I listened eagerly,
And deemed an angel's tongue to hear
   That whispered hope to me,
That heavenly music would be drowned
   In thy harsh, droning voice;
Nor inward thought, nor sight, nor sound,
   Might my sad soul rejoice.

Dull is thine ear, unheard by thee
   The still, small voice of Heaven;
Thine eyes are dim and cannot see
   The helps that God has given.
There is a bridge o'er every flood
   Which thou canst not perceive;
A path through every tangled wood,
   But thou wilt not believe.

Striving to make thy way by force,
   Toil-spent and bramble-torn,
Thou'lt fell the tree that checks thy course,
   And burst through brier and thorn:
And, pausing by the river's side,
   Poor reasoner! thou wilt deem,
By casting pebbles in its tide,
   To cross the swelling stream.

Right through the flinty rock thou'lt try
   Thy toilsome way to bore,
Regardless of the pathway nigh
   That would conduct thee o'er
Not only art thou, then, unkind,
   And freezing cold to me,
But unbelieving, deaf, and blind:
   I will not walk with thee!

Spirit of Pride! thy wings are strong,
   Thine eyes like lightning shine;
Ecstatic joys to thee belong,
   And powers almost divine.
But 'tis a false, destructive blaze
   Within those eyes I see;
Turn hence their fascinating gaze;
   I will not follow thee.

"Coward and fool!" thou mayst reply,
   Walk on the common sod;
Go, trace with timid foot and eye
   The steps by others trod.
'Tis best the beaten path to keep,
   The ancient faith to hold;
To pasture with thy fellow-sheep,
   And lie within the fold.

"Cling to the earth, poor grovelling worm;
   'Tis not for thee to soar
Against the fury of the storm,
   Amid the thunder's roar!
There's glory in that daring strife
   Unknown, undreamt by thee;
There's speechless rapture in the life
   Of those who follow me.

Yes, I have seen thy votaries oft,
   Upheld by thee their guide,
In strength and courage mount aloft
   The steepy mountain-side;
I've seen them stand against the sky,
   And gazing from below,
Beheld thy lightning in their eye
   Thy triumph on their brow.

Oh, I have felt what glory then,
   What transport must be theirs!
So far above their fellow-men,
   Above their toils and cares;
Inhaling Nature's purest breath,
   Her riches round them spread,
The wide expanse of earth beneath,
   Heaven's glories overhead!

But I have seen them helpless, dash'd
   Down to a bloody grave,
And still thy ruthless eye has flash'd,
   Thy strong hand did not save;
I've seen some o'er the mountain's brow
   Sustain'd awhile by thee,
O'er rocks of ice and hills of snow
   Bound fearless, wild, and free.

Bold and exultant was their mien,
   While thou didst cheer them on;
But evening fell,—and then, I ween,
   Their faithless guide was gone.
Alas! how fared thy favourites then,—
   Lone, helpless, weary, cold?
Did ever wanderer find again
   The path he left of old?

Where is their glory, where the pride
   That swelled their hearts before?
Where now the courage that defied
   The mightiest tempest's roar?
What shall they do when night grows black,
   When angry storms arise?
Who now will lead them to the track
   Thou taught'st them to despise?

Spirit of Pride, it needs not this
   To make me shun thy wiles,
Renounce thy triumph and thy bliss,
   Thy honours and thy smiles!
Bright as thou art, and bold, and strong,
   That fierce glance wins not me,
And I abhor thy scoffing tongue—
   I will not follow thee!

Spirit of Faith! be thou my guide,
   O clasp my hand in thine,
And let me never quit thy side;
   Thy comforts are divine!
Earth calls thee blind, misguided one,—
   But who can shew like thee
Forgotten things that have been done,
   And things that are to be?

Secrets conceal'd from Nature's ken,
   Who like thee can declare?
Or who like thee to erring men
   God's holy will can bear?
Pride scorns thee for thy lowly mien,—
   But who like thee can rise
Above this toilsome, sordid scene,
   Beyond the holy skies?

Meek is thine eye and soft thy voice,
   But wondrous is thy might,
To make the wretched soul rejoice,
   To give the simple light!
And still to all that seek thy way
   This magic power is given,—
E'en while their footsteps press the clay,
   Their souls ascend to heaven.

Danger surrounds them,—pain and woe
   Their portion here must be,
But only they that trust thee know
   What comfort dwells with thee;
Strength to sustain their drooping pow'rs,
   And vigour to defend,—
Thou pole-star of my darkest hours
   Affliction's firmest friend!

Day does not always mark our way,
   Night's shadows oft appal,
But lead me, and I cannot stray,—
   Hold me, I shall not fall;
Sustain me, I shall never faint,
   How rough soe'er may be
My upward road,—nor moan, nor plaint
   Shall mar my trust in thee.

Narrow the path by which we go,
   And oft it turns aside
From pleasant meads where roses blow,
   And peaceful waters glide;
Where flowery turf lies green and soft,
   And gentle gales are sweet,
To where dark mountains frown aloft,
   Hard rocks distress the feet,—

Deserts beyond lie bleak and bare,
   And keen winds round us blow;
But if thy hand conducts me there,
   The way is right, I know.
I have no wish to turn away;
   My spirit does not quail,—
How can it while I hear thee say,
   "Press forward and prevail!"

Even above the tempest's swell
   I hear thy voice of love,—
Of hope and peace, I hear thee tell,
   And that blest home above;
Through pain and death I can rejoice.
   If but thy strength be mine,—
Earth hath no music like thy voice,
   Life owns no joy like thine!

Spirit of Faith, I'll go with thee!
   Thou, if I hold thee fast,
Wilt guide, defend, and strengthen me,
   And bear me home at last;
By thy help all things I can do,
   In thy strength all things bear,—
Teach me, for thou art just and true,
   Smile on me, thou art fair!

I have given the last memento of my sister Emily; this is the last of my sister Anne:—

I hoped, that with the brave and strong,
   My portioned task might lie;
To toil amid the busy throng,
   With purpose pure and high.

But God has fixed another part,
   And He has fixed it well;
I said so with my bleeding heart,
   When first the anguish fell.

Thou, God, hast taken our delight,
   Our treasured hope away:
Thou bid'st us now weep through the night
   And sorrow through the day.

These weary hours will not be lost,
   These days of misery,
These nights of darkness, anguish-tost,
   Can I but turn to Thee.

With secret labour to sustain
   In humble patience every blow;
To gather fortitude from pain,
   And hope and holiness from woe.

Thus let me serve Thee from my heart,
   Whate'er may be my written fate:
Whether thus early to depart,
   Or yet a while to wait.

If Thou shouldst bring me back to life,
   More humbled I should be;
More wise—more strengthened for the strife—
   More apt to lean on Thee.

Should death be standing at the gate,
   Thus should I keep my vow:
But, Lord! whatever be my fate,
   Oh, let me serve Thee now!

These lines written, the desk was closed, the pen laid aside—forever.

THE END

CPSIA information can be obtained at www.ICGtesting.com
Printed in the USA
LVOW05s1145071213

364286LV00002B/508/P